THE HOUR
OF THE
PREDATOR

GIULIANO DA EMPOLI is an Italian and Swiss writer and political scientist living in France. He was once a senior advisor to Italian Prime Minister Matteo Renzi. His debut novel, *The Wizard of the Kremlin*, sold more than half a million copies in France, where it also won the Grand Prix du Roman and was a finalist for the Goncourt Prize. It went on to become an international bestseller, being translated into thirty-five languages across the world. A film version, starring Jude Law as Vladimir Putin, is forthcoming. *The Hour of the Predator* has been a no.1 bestseller in France, and translation rights have been sold in eighteen languages so far.

SAM TAYLOR is a translator, novelist and journalist. He is the author of five novels, including *The Two Loves of Sophie Strom*, and the award-winning translator of more than 70 books from French, including David Diop's *Beyond the Door of No Return*, also available from Pushkin Press, Laurent Binet's *HHhH*, Leïla Slimani's *Lullaby* and Hubert Mingarelli's *A Meal in Winter*.

GIULIANO DA EMPOLI

THE HOUR

OF THE

PREDATOR

ENCOUNTERS WITH THE AUTOCRATS
AND TECH BILLIONAIRES TAKING
OVER THE WORLD

TRANSLATED FROM THE FRENCH
BY SAM TAYLOR

PUSHKIN PRESS

Pushkin Press
Somerset House, Strand
London WC2R 1LA

Original text © Éditions Gallimard, Paris, 2025
English translation © Sam Taylor, 2025

First published by Pushkin Press in 2025

ISBN 13: 978-1-80568-016-1

A CIP catalogue record for this title is available from the British Library

The authorised representative in the EEA is
eucomply OÜ, Pärnu mnt. 139b-14, 11317, Tallinn, Estonia,
hello@eucompliancepartner.com, +33757690241

Designed and typeset by Tetragon, London
Printed in the United States of America

www.pushkinpress.com

3 5 7 9 8 6 4 2

'Among the heroes whose
exemplary lives Plutarch recounts,
there are very few gentlemen.'

CURZIO MALAPARTE

WHEN NEWS of Hernán Cortés's arrival first reached the capital of the Aztec Empire, Moctezuma II immediately summoned his closest advisors. How should they react to these unexpected visitors who had appeared out of the blue aboard their strange floating cities?

Some said he should drive back the intruders at once. It wouldn't take the imperial troops long to put an end to a few hundred insolent foreigners who had dared to set foot in the territory of the Triple Alliance. 'Yes, but...' said others. According to the first reports of these foreigners, they seemed to possess supernatural powers: they were completely covered in metal, so that even the sharpest arrows bounced off them. They rode giant deer-like beasts that obeyed their every command. And, most importantly, they had special blowpipes that spat fire and thunder, killing all who opposed their will. What if these beings were not barbarians at all, but gods? And what if their chief—white-skinned, bearded, wearing a shiny helmet—was actually the banished god, the feathered serpent Quetzalcóatl, returning to reclaim his lands?

Caught between these opposing views, the emperor did what politicians throughout human history have done in this sort of situation: he decided not to decide. He sent an embassy to greet the foreigners with gifts, to impress them with the splendour of his reign, but to forbid them to march on the capital. The result of this hesitancy was the same as it has been throughout human history: by risking dishonour in an attempt to avoid war, Moctezuma was left with both war and dishonour.

During the last three decades, the political leaders of Western democracies have, when confronted with the new conquistadors of technology, behaved in exactly the same way as those sixteenth-century Aztecs. Faced with the fire and thunder of the internet, social media and artificial intelligence, they have bowed down—in the hope that some of that magical fairy dust might be sprinkled upon them too.

I cannot tell you the number of times I have witnessed such rituals of degradation. In every capital across the world, the same scene is repeated. The oligarch descends from his private jet, annoyed at being forced to waste his time with this obsolete tribal chief when it could be more usefully employed in some lofty post-human pursuit. After welcoming the oligarch amid great pomp and circumstance, the politician spends a large part of their brief private discussion begging him to build a research centre or an AI laboratory on his territory, before settling for a quick selfie.

As with Moctezuma, their servility has not been enough to ensure our rulers' survival. While pretending to respect the politicians' authority for as long as they found themselves in a position of inferiority, the conquistadors have gradually built their empire. Now the hour of the predator is at hand. And, in this new world, everything that needs to be settled will be settled by fire and sword.

This little book is an account of these events, written from the viewpoint of, and in the style of, an Aztec scribe—using images rather than concepts to capture the dying breath of one world as it sinks into the abyss, and the icy grip of another which will take its place.

NEW YORK, SEPTEMBER 2024

F OUR MEN DRESSED in brown are accompanying the president of the Palestinian Authority. One of them is a little taller than the others, another is a little fatter, but they all have the same grey hair, the same coarse skin, the same worn features of a bureaucrat or a former soldier turned bureaucrat. When they sit down, the hems of their brown trousers rise up to reveal short grey socks that disappear into cheap shoes. While Mahmoud Abbas launches into his monologue on the unfolding tragedy, the men in brown remain perfectly still, their four faces sharing the same expression of vague regret. At a given moment, their boss draws a parallel with the wars of 1948 and 1967, which forced hundreds of thousands of Palestinians into exile. Nobody knows what happened to them then. Some were newborns, then teenagers, tossed who-knows-where by the crashing waves of history. The men's expressions don't change; they are too tired. Nor do they change when the French president begins to speak. One or two of them, perhaps, understand French; the others must wait for the interpreter's translation. But nothing seems to pierce the wall of their exhaustion, even when the conversation between the two heads of state grows more animated.

They remain like that until one particular word is spoken. A single word, unexpected in the flood of all these formulaic phrases, the thousands of words that are habitually spoken in such meetings. When they hear this word, the men in brown become suddenly animated. Their slumped bodies straighten, their dull eyes shine as they look up at the two presidents. The four of them take out little notebooks and start to write, exchanging furtive glances and looking almost happy.

Lula, the president of Brazil, is the ultimate modern embodiment of what Mérimée once observed in Lord Palmerston: 'that mixture of a statesman and a small child'. He gets muddled, calling Macron 'Sarkozy', and he—like the men in brown—has seen too much of life: a metalworker in his teens, thirty years of struggle, prison, then two terms as president, during which he created the Bolsa Família that helped millions of Brazilians out of desperate poverty. And then the fall: prison again, for an absurd scandal, before being acquitted and resurrecting his political career, climaxing with a third term as president at the age of seventy-six. No other world leader can boast of a career like that. Lula is a joker, a world-weary provocateur, but he is still capable of brilliance; he can make his audience laugh and he can make them cry; he can enter a room full of heads of state and bend it to his will.

At the end of the meeting, he mentions Haiti, with its gang-controlled capital, and promises to take care of it. The French president introduces him to the Haitian-Canadian writer Dany Laferrière. Lula smiles enthusiastically, hugging Dany and patting him on the back like some long-lost friend. 'And this is another writer,' Macron tells him, gesturing at me.

A little embarrassed, I say: 'But I'm just an Italian.' Lula laughs, and gives me a consolatory hug.

The Iranian president's bodyguard stands in front of the door to the small room where his boss is in discussion with the French president. An employee of the Élysée Palace's security team goes over to him: 'Sir, you can't stand there.' The Iranian doesn't so much as blink. The Frenchman insists: 'Sir, I can see that you're armed. That's not acceptable. You are on French territory here.'

The Iranian stares at him: 'My president is inside there.'

'So is mine,' the Frenchman replies. 'I can assure you that he is not at risk.'

The Iranian agrees to move a few inches away.

Now it's the turn of the American secret service agent to intervene. 'Sir, you're not allowed to stand there.' Again, the Iranian doesn't blink. 'And I can see that you're armed. That's not acceptable. You are on American territory here.'

For a second, the Frenchman looks lost.

The Iranian steps back to his original position in front of the door.

'Sir, you can't stand there!'

And we're back to square one.

Like the Battle of Waterloo as viewed through the eyes of Fabrice del Dongo in Stendhal's *The Charterhouse of Parma*, the General Assembly of the United Nations is not something that can be seen in its entirety. You need multiple viewpoints to perceive it fully. First, the perspective of the leaders, convinced that they are ruling the world, but more often than not at the mercy of necessity; occasionally they are capable of creating history, but not always in a positive way. Next, the perspective of the negotiators and advisors, or 'sherpas', who weave their webs while exchanging complicit looks, because they know the before and the after, what happens on stage and in the wings. Finally, the perspective of the bodyguards, who stare coldly at each other and struggle with the reality that the whole idea of a security perimeter here is essentially meaningless.

Now, consider these three levels—the leaders, the advisors and the bodyguards—and multiply them by ninety-three, the number of national delegations present at the General Assembly. Each of them utterly convinced that their country is the centre of the world. Yes, even the delegation from Tuvalu. And the one from East Timor. Now you will start to understand why the United Nations cannot function. But perhaps also why we can't do without it.

'On this earth, there is something terrible, and it's the fact that everybody has their reasons.' This observation, from the Jean Renoir film *The Rules of the Game*, finds concrete form in an institution whose purpose is to bring all these reasons into contact with one another. But this is not a theoretical process. The UN General Assembly is, above all, a question of bodies.

The bodies of leaders, accustomed to the vast spaces of the palaces where they normally reside, find themselves squeezed into the narrow corridors and cramped rooms of the misleadingly named Glass Palace. The bodies of advisors and sherpas, perched on their folding seats, listening out for the single word, among all the ritual phrases, that will enable them to move forward, despite the odds stacked against them. And the bodies of body-guards, frustrated at being prevented from doing their job, tensing with irritation or relaxing with philosophical acceptance, running to keep close to their boss, slamming into other bodies.

The body of a powerful person is an abstract entity. Immersed in the pomp of ceremonies that punctuate its existence—the golden sheen of palaces, the sirens of motorcades—it becomes a symbol, the incarnation of a collective entity: the nation, the state. But for this meta-morphosis to work, for a simple human body to become the incarnation of millions of others, space is required: the 'dimensions too considerable for the small number of their guests', the silence and the 'motionless luxury' that Flaubert observed in royal residences.

In Ancient Egypt, the steps leading up to the feet of the pharaoh were higher than necessary so that those who climbed them would feel their inferiority. In Berlin, the New Reich Chancellery built for Hitler by Albert Speer consisted essentially of a corridor almost 500 feet in length that visitors had to walk through before reaching the office with blood-red walls where the Führer awaited them.

Distance, inaccessibility: the more remote the individual, the greater the power of the abstract symbol over the physical body. But the spaces inside the UN's headquarters are too hemmed in, too crowded with powerful people: this year, there are eighty-seven heads of state and twenty-eight government leaders, not to mention all the ministers, ambassadors, heads of international organizations, the European Union, NATO. Consequently, the transfiguration cannot take place, and what remains is the physical body.

The UN General Assembly is the moment, occurring once every year, when the world's most powerful people become mere bodies again.

And all these bodies are in movement. They run through corridors so they can make it to their meetings on time, or at least not be too late. They cram into lifts because they don't want to be left behind. They shove their way through forests of microphones and cameras to reach the packed room where something might be happening. Something they could tell their grandchildren about. Or, more likely, something they'll already have forgotten about by tomorrow morning.

You wait or you run; there is no in-between. This is the rhythm of the General Assembly, and of politics in general. It is deadly boring: as Woody Allen said, ninety per cent of success in life is just showing up. Being there. And then, from time to time, you must pounce.

The provocative theory put forward by the Spanish philosopher José Ortega y Gasset about the state's origins in sport is here startlingly confirmed. Testosterone levels are so elevated that physical confrontations are far from rare.

Particularly since the bodies in question are almost all male. Less than ten per cent of participants in the General Assembly are women. The UN's Secretary-General, António Guterres, deplores this fact once again in his speech, but it is highly unlikely that the situation will change any time soon: the UN itself has never chosen a female leader. Moreover, the men who end up here are not ordinary men. If politics is the continuation of war by other means, it is hardly surprising that this activity tends to attract the most violent characters, people who find meaning in life only when they are in conflict.

Two delegations—each with its leader, its sherpas, its protocol officer, its bodyguards, its secret service agent—charge through a narrow corridor. Each is the centre of the world. Each has a vital meeting that they must (and cannot possibly) attend. They run in opposite directions. They collide. Each delegation expects the other to move out of the way. None of these men are used to yielding; they are accustomed to guards of honour, to roads being closed to traffic, to police cordons sealing them off from any possible hindrance. There are raised voices, outraged expressions. The tension mounts. Hands grab. Shoulders barge. Nostrils flare. Suddenly, the leaders recognize each other. Boric, the Chilean president, is a small wild boar of a man who moves everywhere with such fierce determination that you immediately sense he is incapable of taking a sideways step. He and Macron hug. The conflict is temporarily defused. The delegations go on their way.

*

Ten years ago, when I used to accompany the Italian prime minister on his trips around the world, there was a stupid game that I would play with his spokesman, who was, like me, a big fan of political TV shows. Back then, such series fell into three main categories. The first, which we might describe as heroic, included productions such as *The West Wing*, which represented politics as a virtuous competition between generally competent and well-intentioned people. The second sort of show was darker, depicting politics as a Hobbesian jungle in which nobody is innocent and the only law is survival. This category included *House of Cards*, extremely popular among politicians because it portrayed them as brilliant, unscrupulous Machiavellian characters, leading a fascinating life of intrigues and dirty tricks. The third category, on the other hand, which included sitcoms such as *The Thick of It* and *Veep*—both created by the great Armando Iannucci—showed political life as it actually is: a perpetual comedy of errors in which the characters, almost always unsuited to the positions they occupy, do their best to muddle along, extricating themselves from a series of unexpected, often absurd and sometimes utterly ridiculous situations.

Filippo and I would attempt to work out what percentage of each day we spent travelling corresponded to these three categories. The result was, generally, about 10 per cent *West Wing*, 20 per cent *House of Cards* and 70 per cent *Veep*. At the time, this made us laugh: it was a way of defusing the tension and fatigue that accumulates in such circumstances. Not only that, but the Australian prime minister, Malcolm Turnbull, inadvertently joined our game during the 2016 elections, when he campaigned under the slogan 'Continuity and Change'—almost exactly the same slogan used by the main character for her presidential campaign in season 4 of *Veep*. 'We came up with the most meaningless election slogan we could think of,' explained one of the show's creators.

Since then, the times have changed for the worse. The current global situation offers far fewer opportunities for laughter. Theoretically, the French president's schedule includes a meeting with 'His Excellency Mr Benjamin Netanyahu, Prime Minister of Israel' at 10.15 a.m. on 25 September. But for the past twenty-four hours, in retaliation for a constant barrage of missiles into Israeli territory, the Israeli army has begun a heavy bombardment of southern Lebanon. There have already been hundreds of deaths, and tens of thousands of people have been forced to evacuate their homes to seek shelter further north. Because of this, Netanyahu's presence in New York seems unlikely. It is difficult to make a speech to the UN when you are in the middle of this kind of operation. The French delegation requests an emergency meeting of the Security Council, with the aim of dragging the United States from its pro-longed state of apathy and persuading it to join France in demanding a ceasefire between Israel and Hezbollah.

One essential piece of the puzzle is represented by Iran, the implacable enemy of Israel and the chief sponsor of Lebanese Hezbollah. The Iranian president's minions turn up at the small office occupied by the French to inspect the premises. The last time I saw these men was at the 2015 General Assembly, before the meeting between the Italian prime minister and the Iranian president. That day, they arrived with two Dyson fans, moments before their relaxed, smiling boss entered the room. At the time, the ink had only just dried on the nuclear deal, and relations between the Islamic Republic and the West seemed to be improving.

This time, the atmosphere is different. There are no fans. The advance team perform a meticulous inspection of the room. I don't know what they are searching for. A hidden microphone? A bomb? Maybe even both? Finally, the delegation itself arrives: the president, newly elected after the death of his predecessor in a helicopter accident, the foreign minister and two advisors, all four of them wearing black suits, gleaming beards, blank expressions.

As usual, the meeting takes place on three levels. In the small office, President Pezeshkian recites the litany that he will later repeat to the General Assembly: You Westerners attack us over the smallest things, you are outraged whenever a criminal is thrown in one of our prisons, and at the same time you allow the massacre of thousands of innocent people in Gaza, and now in Lebanon... You should be in uproar against this, not only as political leaders, but first and foremost as human beings.

Meanwhile, in the corridor outside, the bodyguards are dancing the muscular ballet I described at the beginning of this chapter. However, as is often the case in these rigid rituals, the breakthrough happens at an intermediate level, with the sherpas seeking an opportunity that will enable them to restart a dialogue. At the end of the meeting, one of the Iranian sherpas approaches Emmanuel Bonne, the French president's diplomatic advisor. He introduces himself and begins a brief conversation. They take out their business cards. 'Let me give you my mobile number...' Bonne types the number into his own phone. A slender, fragile thread of hope has materialized out of nowhere. Who knows if it will lead to anything.

This is the miracle of the General Assembly: it is the last place where people who are not used to speaking to each other can do so. Except, of course, when they don't turn up. The bilateral meeting with Netanyahu has been officially cancelled. However, the president of Cyprus says the Israeli president is supposed to arrive that night; apparently they are staying in the same hotel. 'The Cypriots are usually pretty well informed,' his French counterpart says, half ironic and half optimistic.

The other spectre haunting the corridors of the Glass Palace is Putin. The Tsar isn't there, but his foreign minister, Sergey Lavrov, thunders from the stage of the General Assembly: 'The hope that Ukraine could defeat Russia on the battlefield is insane, given that Moscow possesses nuclear weapons and that any attempt by the NATO alliance to continue helping Kyiv will prove suicidal.'

France's permanent UN representative tells me about his meetings with Vladislav Surkov—Putin's former spin doctor, who considered himself an artist—during the first negotiations on Ukraine. The character he describes is cold, highly competent and more brutal than I imagined. 'The other Russians would tremble when he came into the room. And he didn't even bother pretending. When we asked about the attitude of the separatists, whom the Kremlin claimed they weren't controlling, he replied: "Don't worry about it, I'll take care of that."' On another occasion, Bonne gave me his description of Surkov: a brutal negotiator who—like many Russians of that kind—could sometimes be physically threatening. But also brilliant, and capable of surprising gestures. 'Now he's gone, all that remains is the brutality,' the diplomat told me with a hint of regret.

Three months before the invasion of Ukraine, Surkov—having recently been fired by Putin—published an article in which he laid bare the truth. Every society, he wrote, is subject to the physical law of entropy. However stable it might be, in the absence of external intervention, it ends up producing chaos within. It is possible to manage the problem up to a certain point, but the only way to solve the issue definitively is to export it. He went on to say that the great empires of history regenerated themselves by sending the chaos they produced beyond their own borders. The Ancient Romans did it, and so—according to Surkov—did the Americans in the twentieth century. And, naturally, so must Russia, 'for whom constant expansion is not merely an idea, but the true existential reason behind our history'.

Like all spin doctors, Surkov does not orchestrate events himself, he just adds a layer of intellectual cynicism to what is happening. To paraphrase Cocteau: 'Since we do not understand these mysteries, let us pretend that we are organizing them.' Not that this makes his thoughts on this matter any less interesting. Anyone who has travelled to the centre of the reactor and is willing to speak about it, however manipulative his words, possesses a quality that those who observe the machine from the outside rarely possess: relevance.

The main victim of the sinister strategy described by Surkov is currently Ukraine. The French president has a face-to-face meeting with Zelensky. This time, there is no space for the sherpas to weave their webs. It is perhaps the most dramatic moment since the start of the war. The Ukrainians are on their last legs. The Russian army, having already suffered the loss of hundreds of thousands of soldiers, is advancing, indifferent to the human cost, and the US election threatens the increasingly uncertain international coalition with imminent implosion.

I don't know what the two leaders said to each other in the basement room where the Ukrainians have their UN office. What I do know is that I have never before seen anything like the scene I witnessed at the meeting's end. After half an hour, Macron opens the door, his face a wax mask. He makes to leave the room: the meeting is over. Just then, Zelensky bursts out after him. Short, muscular, wearing the military fatigues that the whole world has come to recognize, he looks distraught, defeated, on the verge of tears. He grabs Macron's arm and whispers something in his ear. A desperate plea. The French president turns around. He replies. The two men talk for another minute, their bodies close, radiating tension, but nobody can hear what they are saying. Finally, Macron's expression changes: he doesn't smile, but his jaw unclenches. 'That's an idea,' he says. And he leaves Zelensky standing there in the doorway.

Once the chaos goes beyond a certain stage, the only way to restore order is to identify a scapegoat. And the leader, any leader, is always a scapegoat-in-waiting. Tolstoy compared the leader to a ram fattened for slaughter. Fattened on triumph, on the obedience of his subjects, on power and wealth, only to be suddenly struck down by the same force that raised him. I hope Zelensky can escape that fate. But the laws of politics tolerate few exceptions.

The Romans, fine connoisseurs of political tragedy, placed the Tarpeian Rock next to the Capitol. Traitors, sentenced to death, were thrown from its summit only a few yards from the place where they had spent their hours of glory. Nowadays, the principle still remains, even if tragedy often takes the form of farce: 10 per cent *West Wing*, 20 per cent *House of Cards*, 70 per cent *Veep*.

*

I remember two trips to the United States, four months apart. During the first trip—this was October 2016—President Barack Obama had decided to invite his friend Matteo Renzi, then the Italian prime minister, for one last state visit before he had to leave the White House. I remember the guard of honour at the airport, the national anthems, the highway to Washington closed to traffic. We spent the night in the White House. The next morning, the sun was shining on the vast, immaculate lawn, and the American president and his wife were waiting for their Italian counterparts at the top of the front steps. On each step stood a soldier in ceremonial uniform. The sound of trumpets. The boom of nineteen cannon shots. I watched Matteo and his wife with the feeling that this was all vaguely surreal.

Four months later, we found ourselves at the same Washington airport, disembarking from a regular flight.

Everything was slower, more laborious. The man with me, Matteo Renzi, was no longer prime minister, and the border control agent regarded him suspiciously. His colleagues at the immigration department had refused to issue Matteo with an ESTA, the visa waiver that is theoretically granted to anyone with a European passport. 'The fact is that I travelled to Iraq and Iran while I was prime minister.' Matteo smiled. He never lost his sense of irony.

*

In politics, though, it is not only when you fall from grace that you suffer. Politics is a world of perpetual pain. You have to be a certain kind of person to bear it. Like those deep-sea fish that are able to survive the pressure of thousands of tons of water.

Take that hesitant-looking man sitting in the dining room on the fourth floor of the Glass Palace, for a meal that the French delegation are putting on in honour of the community of the Paris Pact for People and the Planet. He is the new British prime minister, Keir Starmer. After the extravagant years of Boris Johnson and the brief period under the rule of the first non-white British leader in history, we now have this polite, smiling, grey-haired, sixty-something London lawyer. He reminds me of Louis

Philippe I, the Citizen King, who famously carried his own umbrella when he walked in the street.

Starmer has not had the easiest of starts. There have been gaffes, riots, budget cuts, even a scandal about his glasses, an expensive pair given to him by a generous donor. The result: two months after his election triumph, the British prime minister's popularity rating is through the floor. No matter what anyone might say about politicians, the fact is that theirs is one of the most difficult jobs in the world. It constantly exposes you to the risk of ridicule. And it can make you look like a total idiot, especially when you are not an idiot at all.

One of Starmer's predecessors, Tony Blair, has just published a book in which he says that political leaders generally go through three stages. First, when they take power, they are willing listeners who know that they don't know everything, and they try to understand how best to interpret their role. After a while, they become convinced that they have gained sufficient experience and they know enough to imagine that they have understood how everything works. This is the most dangerous phrase, when hubris takes hold. 'They're impatient with listening,' Blair writes. 'They're the boss. Who can know more than them?' Finally there is the mature stage, when the leader realizes that his experience does not constitute the sum total of political knowledge and he starts listening to others again. Most leaders, according to Blair, never reach this stage.

The problem is that this kind of existence does not allow you to digest anything. The succession of external impulses is too constant; your brain barely has time to react. It is only once the adventure is over that the politician has the chance to retrace his steps and learn some lessons. If he is even capable of learning such lessons, which is increasingly rare. And if he has not already exploded, like most deep-sea fish do when they're brought towards the surface.

★

The General Assembly Hall is the true architectural masterpiece of the Glass Palace. You can recognize the touch of Oscar Niemeyer, who gave the room, despite its vast size, the tropical elegance of one of his Brazilian creations. I have never, anywhere else in the world, seen such an enormous space that is still able to generate such a feeling of intimacy and comfort. And then there is all the history it contains: the green Prato marble of the rostrum; the golden backdrop, emblazoned with the emblem of the United Nations; the fluted wood walls that everyone has seen a thousand times: on newspaper front pages, on the evening news, in spy films.

A speech given to the General Assembly of the United Nations holds a special place in the world pantheon of political oratory. Think of the rhetorical power of JFK: 'Ladies and gentlemen, the decision is ours. Never have the nations of the world had so much to lose, or so much to gain. Together we shall save our planet, or together we shall perish in its flames.' Or of Fidel Castro who, one year after taking power in Cuba, addressed the Assembly for four and a half hours. And, that same year, Nikita Khrushchev, who took off his shoe and pounded it on the table during a speech by the Philippines delegate. Or Yasser Arafat, who addressed delegates in 1974 with the words: 'Today I have come bearing an olive branch and a freedom fighter's gun. Do not let the olive branch fall from my hand.' And then there was Ronald Reagan, wondering if the only way to unite humanity around a single shared objective would be the threat of an alien invasion.

All these memories make it somewhat disconcerting when you enter the hall and realize that there are only about fifteen people actually listening to the speaker at the rostrum. Sometimes, you might get double that number for a very famous leader. So what is everyone else doing? They are on the phone, or working on their computer, or chatting to their neighbour, or trying to decide whether to go out for sushi or steak later that evening.

This does not, however, mean that the speeches given here have no importance. Quite the contrary, in fact. But the usual rules of oratory don't apply. The objective is not to rouse the audience, but to send out the right signal. And the principle for achieving that is always the same: a few unexpected words that can make all the difference.

At the rostrum of the General Assembly, the French president talks about the risks of an ineffective speech, of powerless diplomacy. Then he attempts to ward off this misfortune by means of one of those memorable phrases. 'We urge Israel to cease escalation in Lebanon, and for Hezbollah to cease missile launches towards Israel. We urge all those who provide them with the means to cease doing so.' *All those who provide the means* for escalation, on both sides. He's dropped the bomb, but the object of his attack—the leaders of the United States, primarily—will pretend they haven't heard.

Macron has a meeting with Joe Biden directly after this speech. The American president comes to the Glass Palace only when he has been asked to address the

General Assembly. The rest of the time he has his own headquarters, at a hotel a few blocks away, and anyone who wants an audience with him must go there.

We enter the lobby of the Barclay, with its atmosphere of the last days before the fall of Saigon. Soldiers, diplomats, henchmen, businessmen, spies. At the bar, people sip whisky, a few have beers, others Coke Zero; after all, it is only three in the afternoon. On the top floor of the hotel, after passing through two additional security checks, we enter a large room with columns and mouldings, wallpaper and deep-pile carpet: everything Americans love. And in the middle of the room, like a funeral bier, is a heavy velvet tent beneath which President Biden conducts his interviews.

All around the room, there's electricity in the air, delegates coming and going. There's even a woman, Ursula von der Leyen, president of the European Commission, small but impeccably neat, giving off the same energy as her male colleagues. But at the centre of this space, there's a void. It's a strange thing to witness. Such a vibrant scene, with a tired old grandfather sitting at its heart, droning on endlessly. He is still here, but everyone else is already thinking about what comes next. He doesn't want to inconvenience anyone, but what is he supposed to do when the planet is on fire? The last transatlantic president, the last Cold War combatant, the last internationalist, and yet the result of his foreign policy is a pile of rubble.

Against all expectations, the French delegation emerges from the Barclay in triumph. The Americans have agreed to support Macron's initiative for an immediate ceasefire in Lebanon. A shiver of excitement runs through the delegation. Could they be at the start of some major new development? In the hours that follow, the European Union, Germany, Italy, Japan, Australia, Canada, Saudi Arabia, the United Arab Emirates and Qatar announce their support for the Franco-American proposal. Is it possible that all this agitation, all these clashes, all these discussions and even all these wrestling matches in corridors might still prove useful—that they are still capable of impacting reality? Rumour has it that Netanyahu is on a plane to New York at that very moment. The Israeli prime minister is expected to speak to the General Assembly on Friday. Everyone is hoping that he will take the opportunity to announce a temporary ceasefire.

At the end of the evening, a feeling of calm satisfaction pervades the French delegation. The president, the ambassador and the advisors all allow themselves a glass of whisky. When these rare *West Wing* moments arrive, they must be savoured. The plan's architect, Emmanuel

Bonne, is in a state of contained euphoria as he looks at the newspaper front pages online, retracing every step of this interminable day and making jokes about how besotted the American president is with Macron's female Middle East advisor.

I think about the words of Alexandre Kojève who, in the late 1940s, risked his status as the most admired philosopher of his generation to become an international negotiator for the French Ministry of Economics. 'I adore this work,' he said. 'For an intellectual, success is a matter of acclaim. You write a book, it gets good reviews or good sales, and that's it. Here, success is a matter of achievement. It gave me such pleasure when my customs system was accepted. It's a higher kind of game.'

Today, though, it is a game that is becoming ever more difficult to play. Hardened gamblers know that the various games in casinos do not all offer the same chance of success. The slot machines give back only 60 per cent of the money they swallow, whereas at the blackjack table a good player can reach 99 per cent. During recent years, the success rate of the sherpas, negotiators and other peacemakers has been in constant decline, as if they have been relegated from the empyrean realms of the green baize tables to the tawdry metallic din of the one-armed bandits.

The next morning, we get a rude awakening. There is no sign of Netanyahu at the UN, and in Lebanon the bombing continues unabated. Another few hours and the situation will finally become clear. The Israeli prime minister will speak to the General Assembly on Friday, and less than an hour later the Israeli air force will raze the block of flats where the Hezbollah leader had his bunker. Some cynics will say that the rumours of Netanyahu's flight to New York were just a ruse to lure Nasrallah into lowering his guard. In this new world, the United Nations is nothing more than a ploy used to strike one's enemies when they least expect it.

When he ordered the Russian army to occupy Crimea in 2014, Putin broke the taboo, laboriously constructed after the Second World War, that forbade countries to use military force to modify their borders. The 2022 invasion of Ukraine rammed home this message in a way that nobody could ignore. War is back in fashion. Leaders who rattle sabres win elections, and some of them follow through on their threats. In the last five years, global military spending has increased by 34 per cent.

All over the world, war fever is catching, and liberal democracies are not immune to the contagion. The United States has moved from the era of hard-fought negotiations among diplomats to that of kinetic diplomacy through military force. In recent years, the illusion that technological supremacy could take the place of in-depth analysis of different local situations in foreign policy has transformed the use of weaponry, physical and digital, from a last resort to an easy first option. In such a context, sophisticated sherpas have become a dying breed. For as long as anyone can remember, career diplomats made up about three-quarters of American ambassadorial appointments, with the remaining quarter being handed out to presidential donors. From 2017, however, Donald Trump reversed this ratio, appointing mostly his own supporters to these positions. His return in 2025 has already shown signs that it might lead to the complete extinction of career ambassadors.

Even in gentle old Europe, anyone who calls for a diplomatic effort is doomed to public scorn, exiled to historical oblivion along with all the once-admired leaders of yesterday's world (the Merkels, the Prodis) and accused of naïvety or, worse, cowardice in the face of the world's inexorable harshness.

Meanwhile, the number of nuclear warheads, which had decreased since the mid 1980s, has started to rise again: China is building hundreds of missile silos in its northern deserts; North Korea's nuclear missiles are aimed at cities on the West Coast of the United States; Iran is closer than ever to becoming a nuclear power; and the threat of Russian nuclear weapons looms over the end of the Ukraine war. The Doomsday Clock, updated every year by the successors of the physicists behind the Manhattan Project, is now set at eighty-nine seconds to midnight, the closest humanity has ever come to extinction since the clock was created in 1947.

FLORENCE, MARCH 2012

I<small>N ANOTHER LIFE</small>, I took part in a scientific project intended to discover, behind the immense frescoes that Vasari painted on the walls of the Hall of the Five Hundred in Florence's Palazzo Vecchio, the traces of Leonardo da Vinci's *The Battle of Anghiari*.

That artwork was never finished, and all that remains of it are some preparatory drawings. Leonardo had been given the task of covering the hall's eastern wall with a representation of a glorious episode from Florence's past: the moment when the republic's army defeated the Duke of Milan who was, with the aid of exiled Florentine aristocrats, attempting to seize the city.

While the scientists calibrated their machines around Vasari's fresco, I imagined Leonardo, bearded and alone, perched on some scaffolding not so different to our own, doing his work surrounded by blazing fires. For *The Battle of Anghiari*, the artist had decided to use the ancient technique of encaustic painting, applying the heated colours directly to the wall, then fixing them with the aid of strange metal tools.

His intention was not to glorify war, but to show it in all its brutality. A few years before this, he had witnessed Charles VIII's military expedition, which had brought to Italy a ferocity of warfare unseen in centuries.

While the Italian city states had long neglected the art of war, entrusting the settling of their differences to armies of foreign mercenaries, the French, hardened by the Hundred Years' War against England, possessed a large and powerful national army. Unlike the Italian forces, which tended to respect civilian populations and not inflict unnecessary damage on territories that they would later have to govern, the French were already adept at total warfare. So whenever they seized a village or a stronghold, they would ruthlessly annihilate it. The Italian historian Francesco Guicciardini has left us a horrified account of the taking of Monte San Giovanni, when all its inhabitants were executed and the village set ablaze.

War is, above all, a matter of chaos and destruction. Which is why Leonardo chose to represent the confrontation as a savage melee of godless, lawless men, more like a pack of wild beasts than the noble combat of two national armies. 'First show the smoke of the artillery mingled in the air with the dust raised by the movement of horses and soldiers,' he wrote in his notebook, describing the atmosphere he wished to depict. 'Arrows will rise in all directions, descending, flying in straight lines, filling the air, and musket balls will leave a trail of smoke in their wake.'

Thirteen years ago, despite all our efforts, we were not able to find the traces of this fresco on the walls of the Palazzo Vecchio. But now, it's as if the martial fury depicted by Leonardo is palpable behind every news story, as if the artillery smoke from the Battle of Anghiari has permeated the air that we breathe.

In Libya, in the Middle East, in Ukraine: the edges of the continent that made peace the foundation of its reconstruction are being transformed into one vast battlefield. And every day, the war creeps ever further inside Europe's borders. Russian agents have, in recent months, been suspected of assassinating a defector in Spain, setting fire to malls and warehouses in several countries, planting parcel bombs on cargo planes, and the attempted murder of the CEO of one of Germany's biggest arms consortiums. Not to mention the large-scale disinformation campaigns that are increasingly being transformed into full-on cyber-attacks. The media do not always have access to all the facts, but polling stations in most European countries, for example, are systematically targeted by Russian hackers whenever there is a local or national election.

This explosion of violence corresponds to a pattern long observed by military historians. There are phases in history when defensive techniques progress more quickly than offensive techniques. During these periods, wars become rarer because the cost of attacking is higher than the cost of defending. But there are other times when offensive technologies gain the upper hand. These are the bloodiest ages, when wars break out more frequently, because attacking others is cheaper than defending what you have. During Leonardo da Vinci's lifetime, the spread of artillery throughout Europe brought the continent out of a relatively peaceful period, when most assaults foundered against fortress walls, and into a new and more violent era, when cast-iron cannonballs gave the advantage to the aggressors. This went on until, in response to numerous French incursions, Italian architects developed a new construction style—bastion forts—that enabled fortresses to resist artillery assaults. It was at this point, the relationship between offensive and defensive technologies having regained a certain equilibrium, that defence took over again and peace was restored, more or less. After this, the development of mobile artillery—cannons capable of opening breaches in the most solid fortifications—gave the advantage back to the aggressors. New wars followed. And so on, until the modern day.

In the wake of the Second World War, and throughout the Cold War, the nuclear deterrent made the cost of any large-scale attack prohibitive. But the evolution of the geopolitical context and the progress of technology brought an end to this period of relative calm: the attack on the Twin Towers, which resurrected history after the premature announcement of its death, cost less than a million dollars to organize. Today, an aircraft carrier on which the American government spent $10 billion can be sunk by two or three Chinese-made hypersonic missiles that cost only $15 million. On the other hand, to bring down a $200 drone launched by the Houthis in the Red Sea, the US and allied forces have to use missiles costing millions of dollars. And that's without even taking into account that a cyber-attack capable of paralysing an entire nation can be launched practically for free.

These days, attack is cheaper than defence. Much cheaper. And the price keeps coming down. In the future, some believe, a single individual will be able to declare war on the rest of the world—and win. When you bear in mind that a DNA synthesizer with the potential to create fatal new pathogens costs about $20,000—the price of a used car—this does not seem especially far-fetched.

Even according to the company that produces it, the latest ChatGPT model, launched in the autumn of 2024, has caused a significant increase in the risk that artificial intelligence could be used by bad actors to create chemical, biological, radiological and nuclear weapons. The company's own scale now classifies the risk at the highest possible level, but this has not prevented OpenAI from putting the product on the market, and no regulatory authority has raised any objections.

In Leonardo da Vinci's time, the old institutions—the small city states and republics that were scattered across the Italian peninsula—almost all succumbed to the violence unleashed by the new technology. A few years after Leonardo's attempt to paint *The Battle of Anghiari* in the Hall of the Five Hundred, the Republic of Florence ceased to exist as a political entity. And for centuries afterwards, the peninsula became little more than a battlefield for foreign powers. The Italians had to wait until the second half of the nineteenth century to regain their independence.

Today, our democracies appear more solid. But nobody can doubt that the toughest test is yet to come.

The new American president is at the head of a motley procession of shameless autocrats, tech conquistadors, reactionaries and conspiracy theorists, all spoiling for a fight. An era of limitless violence lies ahead of us, and, as in Leonardo's time, the defenders of freedom seem singularly unprepared for the battle to come.

'THE CROWN PRINCE is a very sweet man,' one of his friends tells me as we pass through the metal detector at the Ritz-Carlton in Riyadh. And who could doubt it, observing this amiable man while he welcomes the CEOs of a dozen major companies in a small room inlaid with marble, onyx and jasper that looks like something from *One Thousand and One Nights*? He smiles constantly, and his smile is disarmingly sweet, almost childlike—the same smile you can see in the few images of the prince in his youth, when Mohammed bin Salman was merely one Saudi prince among hundreds, back when he had to make people like him just to get noticed. He has the stature of a giant, but he's a friendly giant, with a bear-like physique that seems made for hugging people. His bodyguards appear nervous: they are the crown prince's last defence, after the metal detectors at the entrance, after the two rows of warriors in white dishdashas with their unsheathed sabres in the corridor, after the ante-chamber bristling with green-uniformed, single-headed Cerberuses. But MBS, as he is known, is all sweetness and light. Being in his presence is like reaching an oasis of serenity. His guests line up to be introduced to him. MBS has a smile and an encouraging word for each of them. In this small room that resembles a chapel with all its gold, mother-of-pearl and marquetry, I feel as though I am attending a first communion. Or, more pertinently perhaps, a baptism.

Ever since the rise of MBS, the cult of the future has become the main religion of Saudi Arabia. The new linear city, 110 miles long and 660 feet wide, which is supposed to house nine million inhabitants and to be powered entirely by renewable energy; the winter sports resort that will host the 2029 Asian Winter Games; the octagonal floating port projected to be thirty-three times the size of New York City; Expo 2030, to be held in Riyadh; its new airport and new airline; the gargantuan projects for green hydrogen, robots and, of course, artificial intelligence... It's all happening here, at the command of this sweet, smiling prince.

And yet there is one detail that worries me. This place. The Ritz-Carlton is by far the most luxurious hotel in the Saudi capital. This is where visiting heads of state, tech princes and touring celebrities always stay. This is the setting for 'Davos in the Desert', an economic forum that the crown prince has hosted every year since 2017. But the businessmen who booked a room on 4 November that year were in for a nasty surprise. Overnight, their reservations were cancelled. Worse still, the guests already in the hotel were abruptly told to leave, and a message announcing the hotel's closure for an indefinite period appeared on the palace website. Which does not mean that the hotel lay empty—only that MBS had decided to organize a very different kind of party there.

Back then, MBS was not yet quite the sweet prince that he would later become. Having been named the heir to the Saudi throne four months earlier, at the age of thirty-one, he was surrounded by jealous uncles and cousins, most of whom possessed unlimited resources, including whole sectors of the state, ministries and police forces. His position still appeared precarious. Some gossips even whispered that the previous crown prince's abdication had not been quite as spontaneous as was suggested; that his decision had perhaps been influenced by a long night of captivity at the royal palace in the company of MBS's henchmen.

In early November, some 300 of the richest and most powerful men in the kingdom received the kind of offer that cannot be refused. The invitations were personalized. Some came from the old king Salman, eighty-one years old and in poor health, others directly from his son Mohammed. Some of the letters were vague about the reason for the summons, while others gave precise explanations: for example, Prince Miteb, head of the 120,000-strong National Guard, was informed that a Yemeni missile had landed in the suburbs of Riyadh; others were lured with the promise of lucrative business offers. The tone of the letters brooked no argument: each addressee was ordered to present himself immediately to the royal palace.

But when they arrived at the palace, the royal guards first separated them from their security details, then confiscated their telephones, wallets and identity papers. Next, these VIPs were taken to the Ritz-Carlton, where they were informed that they would be guests of the crown prince for an indefinite period. When they woke the next morning, courteous officials brought each of the 300 princes, governors and billionaires a set of twelve white T-shirts, twelve pairs of white boxer shorts, twelve pairs of white socks, three djellabas and three sets of pyjamas. It looked like they were in for the long haul.

In a suite of the Ritz-Carlton, with its Empire-style furniture, its damask walls and its crystal chandeliers, I try to imagine the faces of those princes, ministers and billionaires of royal blood when they were handed those neatly folded white clothes. The more astute among them must have realized in that moment that they had entered a new reality. Perhaps some of them felt relieved: there is sometimes a certain comfort to be found in being relieved of one's responsibilities, in the passage from freedom to constraint. Others, it is true, might have taken it badly. Prince Al-Waleed, for example, was used to a particular lifestyle. Ranked by *Forbes* among the fifty wealthiest people on the planet, he was forever travelling in one of his three private jets between the Savoy in London and the various hotels in the Four Seasons chain (of which he was the principal shareholder). And when he was in Riyadh, Prince Al-Waleed would generally receive visitors while sitting on a throne in the penthouse on the ninety-ninth floor of the Kingdom Center Tower (which he owned), surrounded by models wearing lingerie (which he himself had designed). Prince Salman, on the other hand, had more refined tastes. Educated at Oxford and the Sorbonne, he traversed the planet in search of works of art, which he distributed among his villas in the south of France and his six mega-yachts from the Lürssen shipyard in Bremen.

For all of these men—princes, members of the government and billionaires (and quite a few of the prisoners ticked all three boxes)—the delivery of the white clothing was followed by the first interrogations. And at this point, it is true, the situation became a little less aseptic, MBS having decided, in his infinite sweetness, to invite the mercenaries of the notorious Blackwater security service to assist his bodyguards in their conversations with the captives. From then on, for three months, these Ritz-Carlton rooms more used to the clink of glasses containing non-alcoholic Bellinis were filled with the tears, yelps and muffled screams of princes and billionaires subjected to the muscular interrogations of Gulf War veterans. Each of them was presented with evidence (of varying degrees of veracity) of his corrupt acts, before being urged, verbally and sometimes physically, to agree to MBS's conditions for acquittal.

Of course, none of this excludes the possibility that the crown prince is a very sweet man. But it does suggest that he bears more than a little resemblance to the kind of prince once depicted by Machiavelli.

On the night of 31 December 1502, the obscure Florentine secretary Niccolò Machiavelli found himself in Senigallia, on the Adriatic coast, where he had been sent as an envoy to Cesare Borgia, known as the Duke of Valentinois, who had just recaptured his duchy after being confronted with a conspiracy of his former allies, Vitellozzo Vitelli, Oliverotto da Fermo and the Orsini brothers.

That night, all was harmony. After intense negotiations a truce had been reached, enabling the duke to regain possession of his territories. To seal the settling of their differences, Borgia, Vitelli and the others decided to seize the fortress of Senigallia and to celebrate the New Year there with an extravagant banquet. Borgia got there first but, as a gesture of courtesy, chose to wait for the others before making his triumphal entrance into the town. When they arrived, he went up to each of these men who, three months earlier, had wanted him dead, and embraced them like brothers. Only one—Oliverotto—was missing, so the duke dispatched a messenger to invite him to join them. It would be a shame for him to miss this, Borgia said. He wanted them all to enter the town together, amid great pomp, to celebrate their reconciliation. And that's just what they did, preceded by the heavy cavalry and the Swiss guards. Inside the palace, a magnificent feast awaited them. At a certain point in the evening, when the *condottieri*, tired from their merrymaking, sought permission to retire for the night, Borgia asked them to accompany him to a private room where they could discuss their future plans: the capture of Senigallia was just the beginning! Soon after this, though, the duke made some excuse and slipped away. Barely had he left than a gang of armed men surrounded the guests and arrested them. Then Borgia's troops disarmed Oliverotto's men and pillaged the town. Machiavelli, a witness to these events, wrote to his masters in the Florentine government that, in his opinion, none of the prisoners would survive the night. When dawn broke the following day, he was proved only half right: Oliverotto and Vitelli had been strangled, but the Orsinis were still alive. In deference to their princely blood, they would be granted a stay of execution, meeting their fate two weeks later.

Events at the Ritz-Carlton had a slightly less violent denouement, although it's true that one of the captives did pass away during an overly enthusiastic interrogation. The others escaped with their lives. The head of the National Guard was dismissed and forced to sign a cheque for a billion dollars in return for his freedom. Prince Al-Waleed was relieved of $6 billion after being waterboarded. He now has to wear an electronic bracelet and is not allowed to leave the kingdom. Still, he is better off than some others, including Prince Turki bin Abdullah, the former governor of Riyadh, who is still in prison now.

All in all, the party at the Ritz-Carlton allowed the Saudi state to recover more than $8 billion to fund the young prince's ambitious projects. Most importantly, the operation cut off the heads of the hydra that was threatening MBS's domination. For a princely elite used to palace intrigues on a smaller scale, with the country's most powerful men peacefully coexisting in order to maintain an impenetrable façade of unity, this was a deeply shocking episode. And since that time, these men—among the most pampered on the planet—have probably not known a night's peace. Once the germ of fear starts to grow, it spreads quickly, nourished by memories of those luxury hotel suites transformed into torture chambers.

'Men are either to be kindly treated or utterly crushed, since they can revenge lighter injuries, but not graver. Wherefore the injury we do to a man should be of a sort to leave no fear of reprisals.' Ten years after that night in Senigallia, Machiavelli would make Cesare Borgia the model for *The Prince*: not the ideal ruler, but the beast of real power, half fox and half lion, cunning enough to flatter men and forceful enough to subjugate them.

Five centuries later, MBS is Borgia 2.0. Like the Renaissance duke, who nurtured a grandiose ambition of unifying Italy under his rule, MBS has outlined a strategic vision of transforming Saudi Arabia into a powerful, modern nation, freed from the grip of religious fundamentalism, with power concentrated in his hands. As with his Italian forebear, however, the Saudi prince's status remains fragile, vulnerable to a reversal of fortune.

In that chapel-like room of the Ritz-Carlton, I feel like I can catch an ironic gleam, now and then, in the prince's eyes. As if the constraints of protocol were masking a parallel reality, glimpsed only in odd moments, in the sly looks that MBS exchanges, when he thinks no one is watching, with the few members of his entourage that really matter: his brother Khaled, the defence minister; Prince Bader, minister of culture; Fahad Toonsi, head of the department in charge of the prince's mega-projects. All these men are young—most of them under forty—and are currently in positions of astonishing power that none of them had been expected to reach. With his Ritz-Carlton power play, MBS has overturned the geronto-cracy that governed Saudi Arabia for decades, enabling these younger men to rise to power with him. Imagine the euphoria they must have felt, these men—and others whom we do not see, like Saud Al-Qahtani, the evil genius commanding a cyber-army of trolls, or Turki Al-Sheikh, the former bodyguard now promoted to the grand vizier of the court—when the doors of the Al Yamamah Palace banged shut and the last of the grey-haired officials had left the building. I imagine them like a group of rich teenagers going crazy in a villa after their parents have left town, gobbling Wagyu hamburgers, playing *Call of Duty* and bringing in call girls from London and Dubai, amid the jubilant, almost disbelieving atmosphere that follows a wildly ambitious and somehow successful bank robbery.

Thinking about it, there is probably nothing strange about the idea of MBS being the reincarnation of Cesare Borgia 500 years later, because the moment we are living through is similarly Machiavellian. During the period when Leonardo was painting and inventing, it was the Florentine secretary who sounded the death knell for illusions. The sophisticated world of the humanists, with their principles and their rules, the endless factional quarrels poisoning the politics of his homeland: none of this made any sense when faced with the geometrical firepower of foreign invaders. The author of *The Prince* didn't care about the norms of legitimate power because they no longer corresponded to the reality that he saw around him. What interested Machiavelli was trying to understand how power can be asserted amid chaos, when everyone is fighting everyone else and force becomes, once again, the only rule of the game. Inheriting a principality is easy. What is much more difficult is illegitimately conquering one and, most importantly, keeping it.

The Prince is a usurper's guide to conquering and ruling. There are many lessons to be drawn from its pages for Borgias of all eras, but one of them stands out above all the others: the first law of strategy is action. In a situation of uncertainty, when the legitimacy of power is precarious and can be called into question at any moment, he who fails to act can be sure that change will happen anyway—to his disadvantage.

If Tolstoy shows us that the condition of the powerful man is always to be thwarted, since the fulfilment of his will depends on the will of so many other people that it becomes practically impossible, meaning that the lowest infantryman in Napoleon's army has more freedom than the emperor himself, then the resolute action of a prince constitutes the solution to this problem.

This is what today's Kremlin insiders call 'manual override'. When the system, with all its procedures and hierarchies, no longer produces the desired result, there remains the possibility of direct intervention: breaking the official rules to re-establish substantive justice. What comes from this is a form of miracle, in the literal meaning of the word, since a miracle is the direct intervention of God upon Earth.

But for the miracle of power to happen, it takes more than a resolute action. The action must also be reckless, because what is the point of an action that simply responds to necessity? That would be little more than the act of a technocrat, one of those cruel, grey functionaries who act in the name of constraints from on high, which they claim only they can control. The essence of power resides in the very opposite of this. Goethe tells the story of an old Saxon duke, intuitive and wilful, who was urged to think carefully before making an important decision. 'I don't want to think carefully,' he replied. 'Otherwise, what would be the point of being Duke of Saxony?'

The apogee of power coincides not so much with action as with reckless action, which is the only kind that will shock people. And shock is the foundation of the prince's power. When the Lebanese prime minister Saad Hariri landed in Riyadh in the autumn of 2017, the last thing he was expecting was to be imprisoned and coerced into resigning his position. When the *Washington Post* reporter Jamal Khashoggi entered the Saudi consulate in Istanbul to renew his passport, the last thing he expected was to be strangled, taken down to the basement and dismembered with a saw. When the owner of Amazon, Jeff Bezos, received a friendly WhatsApp message from the Saudi crown prince, the last thing he expected was for his phone to be hacked by a piece of Israeli spy software that harvested the most embarrassing details of his private life so that they could then be made public. And yet all these surprises—and many others—did occur, at the behest of MBS, the crown prince who might be as sweet as everyone says, but who is also as ruthless as a Borgia.

NEW YORK, SEPTEMBER 2024

T HE MARBLE ROSTRUM of the General Assembly is accustomed to hosting the most varied of garbs. The multicoloured outfits worn by African presidents, the elaborate hairstyles of Asian sovereigns, the arcane geometries of military uniforms: all of these reflect the variety of customs on the planet and make not the slightest impression on the jaded audience in the Glass Palace. The closest anyone has ever come to making a splash was a few years ago, when the corrupt Afghan president's elegantly flowing silk capes and astrakhan hat provoked some approving nods among the few aesthetes present.

A less common occurrence is for a head of state to appear dressed in an outfit of his own invention, made for him by Miss Universe's stylist. Yet this is what happened when Nayib Bukele, the young president of El

Salvador, appeared in an indigo tunic with golden floral motifs embroidered on the cuffs and collar, giving him a look midway between Simón Bolívar and a *Star Wars* character. This was also how he dressed in early summer, during his second inauguration, in the presence of the king of Spain and Donald Trump Jr. On that occasion, the imposing honour guard of cadets from the Escuela Militar de San Salvador had also been given a new look by Miss Universe's stylist, who had dressed each of its members in a cape notable for its length and beauty, but perhaps not for its suitability to the tropical temperatures of a Saturday in June.

On the UN rostrum Bukele stands alone, but the military tunic, combined with his upstanding posture, gives him an appealingly heroic look. 'The coolest dictator in the world,' as he described himself in response to a tweet from Kamala Harris, who was expressing concerns over the summary methods he had used to tackle the problem of crime in his country. He has also called himself a 'philosopher king', in his biography on X, while some foreign newspapers have nicknamed him the 'millennial Caudillo'. When he was elected for the first time, at the age of thirty-seven, El Salvador was the most violent country in the world: the homicide rate there was three times higher than in Haiti, considered a bankrupt state.

Bukele's response was radical: he replaced the penal code with an illustrated tattoo manual.

In El Salvador, as in Japan and Russia, gang members—*pandilleros*—recognize one another from the symbols they wear on their skin: an Aztec sun, a Kalashnikov, the face of a laughing madman intended to represent the gangster's *vida loca*. Two years ago, after another massacre, Bukele proclaimed a state of emergency and ordered the army to arrest anyone with tattoos.

The result: 80,000 people were imprisoned, most of them criminals, but a few just rock fans who'd made the mistake of getting inked. Next, since the millennial Caudillo was originally a publicist, he had videos shot of gangsters (and those unfortunate rock fans) in boxer shorts, heads shaved, tattoos gleaming in the spotlights, forced to their knees in their thousands in the corridors of the new, high-security Tecoluca prison, or running in tight ranks to the guards' whistles. Part *Hunger Games* and part gay porn movie, these videos were naturally a big hit on social media, turning Bukele into the head of state with the highest number of TikTok followers.

Of course, Amnesty International and other humanitarian NGOs did not appreciate Bukele's methods, but the fact is that the homicide rate is now ten times lower than it was before, making El Salvador the safest country in the West, above even Canada.

Which is why Bukele is now standing on the UN rostrum: 'Some say we've imprisoned thousands of people, but the truth is that we have liberated millions. Now it's the good guys who can live without fear.' At this line, I see the French president's speech-writer, Baptiste Rossi, sit up in his seat. You see, at least some people in the General Assembly Hall are paying attention: the global brotherhood of speech-writers is always on the lookout for winning phrases, and no matter how far apart they may be politically, one artist can always appreciate another's work. From this purely technical viewpoint, Bukele is one of the best orators around.

El Milagro Bukele, as it is known throughout Latin America, is another miracle of the age. Like MBS, the president of El Salvador is a fan of Borgian action: the combination of an audacious idea with expeditious means to create a divine surprise. Unlike the Saudi prince, however, Bukele did not rise to power within an autocratic system but in a democracy, whose limits he is testing.

When the Salvadorean parliament threatened to reject his anti-crime plan in 2020, Bukele turned up at the chamber escorted by the army before announcing, in a speech to the partisan mob outside, that if the plan was rejected he would not intervene to save the corrupt deputies from the righteous wrath of the people. Next, he fired every judge in the country aged sixty or over and replaced them with his own supporters. Then, thanks to a new interpretation of the constitution, he stood for re-election to the presidency, which was theoretically impossible.

The election finally took place in February 2024, in the presence of more than 3,000 international observers who certified its absolute regularity. The millennial Caudillo was re-elected with 84 per cent of the vote, and his party, Nuevas Ideas, which hadn't even existed six years before, won fifty-four of the sixty seats in parliament. 'This is not a one-party state,' Bukele remarked. 'This is a democracy with one dominant party. In all democracies, the leaders' objective is to win as much as possible. Do you think that during elections in France or the United States, the president says: "Let's try not to get more than 55 per cent of the votes so we can maintain the balance of power"? Of course they don't. The objective of all leaders is to obtain as many votes as possible. They fail, but their failure cannot be my road map. What was I supposed to do? Announce that, since all the other presidents are failing, since they're all unpopular, I'll also give half of the seats to the opposition just so we're the same as all the other countries?'

'HA HA HA, I'M BACK!' Donald Trump made several phone calls to foreign heads of state, starting each with a triumphant laugh and this menacing announcement. Some of the people he called must have felt a little uncomfortable, but that is not the case for Bukele. For him, Trump's return to office is proof that he was right all along. And that all those who believed Trumpism was a passing phase, an accident of history, were wrong.

The day after Trump's victory, Bukele wrote on X: 'No matter your political preference or whether you like what happened or what's yet to happen […] I'm certain you don't fully grasp the fork in human civilization that began yesterday.' One month before this, the Republican candidate had given a speech in Erie, Pennsylvania, in which he outlined a solution to the problem of juvenile delinquency copied straight from the one used in El Salvador.

'You see these guys walking out with air conditioners, with the refrigerators on their back, the craziest thing,' said Trump, never short of colourful images, as he addressed a crowd including a surprisingly large proportion of people in mirror sunglasses. 'And the police aren't allowed to do their job. They're told, "If you do anything, you're going to lose your pension. You're going to lose your family, your house, your car." The police want to do it. […] They're not allowed to do it because the liberal Left won't let them do it. The liberal Left wants to destroy them, and they want to destroy our country. If you had one day, like one real rough, nasty day […] one rough hour, and I mean real rough, the word will get out and it will end immediately.'

The idea of a day without rules, similar to the strategy employed by Bukele, was greeted with roars of approval by Trump's supporters. Here at last was someone willing to rip into the criminals, after all these politicians who seemed to be more on their side than on the side of the people being robbed.

The same goes for the idea of cutting government expenses with a chainsaw, eliminating entire departments in the American administration, which Trump ripped off wholesale from the Argentine president Javier Milei, before entrusting the execution of the plan to the world's richest man, Elon Musk.

*

There was a time when political innovation radiated out from the centre. In the United States, someone proposed a new idea, led a different kind of campaign: a striking slogan, a new way of using the media, of addressing voters. It started from there, from California, from Madison Avenue or K Street, and then, slowly, innovation extended to the margins. In Britain, someone noticed this and began aping the Americans, then the innovation spread to the Scandinavian countries, to Germany, to the rest of Europe, and—little by little—the future of political communication spread all over the world, to the furthest reaches of Asia and Africa.

I remember those pilgrimages in the 1990s and early 2000s, in the heart of this dull, imperial city, in the small windowless rooms used by think-tanks, with their carpet tiles in that indefinable colour midway between grey and brown, and their trays of stale cookies and muffins, where we believed we were riding the zeitgeist into a beautiful future, because everything seemed to be heading in the right direction.

Now everything has changed. In the fields of political communication and propaganda, the trajectory of political innovation has been reversed. What's new no longer goes in one direction, from the centre to the periphery, as it did before. More and more, these days, it comes from unlikely places or it is tested on the periphery before moving to the centre.

Ten years ago, Cambridge Analytica paved the way by importing into Europe and the United States the information war techniques it had developed for the British army and intelligence services in Pakistan and Colombia. In a world where the digital condition has become the first truly global experience, shared by the entire population of the world, the dynamics of the internet and social media can be exploited in more or less the same way everywhere. So Nigeria, for example, might become a perfect testing ground for a campaign in Norway.

When political competition took place in the real world, in public squares and on traditional media, each country's customs and regulations could determine its limits, but now that it has moved online, public debate has become a free-for-all where everything is permitted and the only rules are those imposed by the platforms. Consequently, the fate of our democracies is being played out increasingly in a sort of digital Somalia, a bankrupt state the size of the planet, at the mercy of the overlords of online warfare and their militias. Nowadays, it is not only communication techniques but rallying cries, content and programmes that are circulating freely from seminars at the Danube Institute in Budapest to NatCon conferences in Miami to Buenos Aires.

What has changed from the way it was eight years ago is that the pedestal on which the old order stood has collapsed. In the mid 2010s, Trump, Bolsonaro and the Brexiters were able to appear like a group of outsiders, defying the established order and adopting a strategy of chaos, like guerrilla insurgents battling a superior force. Now the situation has been reversed: chaos is no longer the weapon of the rebels, but the banner of those in power.

While in the West the first half of the twentieth century taught politicians the virtues of restraint, the passing of the last generation to have experienced world war has enabled the return of demiurges who are reinventing reality and claiming to mould it to their will.

All the guardrails of the old world—the respect for the independence of certain institutions, human and minority rights, a concern for international repercussions—have no value now that the hour of the predator is upon us.

In this new world, every process will be driven to its most extreme consequences. Nothing will be contained or governed. The brake lines have been cut. *Pedal to the metal* has become the only possible option.

The window of opportunity that existed until recently for a system of rules to be put in place has now closed. The very idea of a limit to the logic of force, finance or crypto-currency, to the growing power of AI and technological convergence, or to the upending of the international order in favour of the law of the jungle, is no longer conceivable.

In this new era, the Borgians have an advantage because they are used to existing in a world without limits. They are not content to resist adversity; they draw their strength from instability, unpredictability, aggression.

Donald Trump is a life form perfectly adapted to the present moment. One of his traits—which his advisors, still in thrall to old-fashioned norms, complain about in whispers, when they really ought to openly boast about it—is that he never reads. To his mind, books are museum pieces, and newspapers are heading the same way. Anyone who saw a photograph of Trump on his private jet or in an armchair at Mar-a-Lago with a book in his hands would have to be ludicrously naïve not to immediately suspect it of being a deepfake. What worries his advisors—and again, they ought to be rejoicing at this fact—is that Trump won't even read the page or half-page of notes that they hand him in preparation for a meeting, summarizing the fundamental issues of the subject at hand. Trump won't even glance at those notes. Not a page, not a half-page, not a single line. He only processes information orally. Which represents a considerable challenge for anyone trying to transmit any sort of structured knowledge.

But why should that matter, when the truly important thing is action? Because knowledge is the enemy of action. A chaotic environment demands bold decisions that captivate the public attention and shock his adversaries.

When it comes down to it, Trump is merely yet another illustration of one of the obvious, unchanging principles of politics: there is practically no connection between intellectual power and political intelligence. The world is full of highly intelligent people—even among political specialists and experts—who understand absolutely nothing about politics, whereas a functional illiterate like Trump has a sort of natural genius for interpreting the zeitgeist.

How many billionaire businessmen, global technocrats, intellectuals and Nobel Prize winners have we seen humiliate themselves trying to translate their professional success into the political arena?

According to the modest calculations of this Aztec scribe, there are, at any given moment, 123 people in Paris who believe they have a serious chance of becoming the next president of France. Among them, seven or eight actually have a chance. The others know that they are not in a position of strength, but they tell themselves: you never know, maybe some unforeseen combination of circumstances will lead to the historical necessity of their rise to power.

All over the planet, brilliant men and women always start in the same way, puffed up with pride, convinced that they have already done the hard work by using their undoubted talents to triumph in the highly competitive worlds of business, diplomacy, culture or science. How difficult could politics be in comparison? After all, politicians are just a bunch of characters in search of an author, bereft of any professional skills, barely capable of stringing two words together. Right?

No sane person would get involved in this shady underworld. But these intellectuals have decided it is time to elevate the tone: after all, if the good guys never enter the arena, the situation will never improve.

And so they test the water, start giving interviews, distilling their ideas into a book, founding a think-tank or accepting a direct invitation from a political party to stand for election. And then, at some point, they make a horrible discovery.

They realize that all this is way more difficult than they'd thought. Not because the arena is full of geniuses, but because there is no arena, there are no rules, there are not even any stable points of reference. And yet a game does exist. A game that very few people are able to play. Questioned after the Congress of Berlin in 1878, the Prussian statesman Bismarck replied—in a high-pitched voice that would have made it impossible for him to achieve any kind of political success today—that his job consisted of juggling five balls, keeping two of them constantly in the air. If the Iron Chancellor considered nineteenth-century politics a circus act, I will let you imagine what it has become in a less structured context.

As the Chinese say, power is a dragon in the fog. To hunt it is to be confronted, every day, with feelings of futility, uncertainty, contradiction. *Veep* is a useful touchstone, but to gain a more accurate picture, you should throw in *Squid Game* and *The Godfather*, a film whose script has been memorized by practically every political animal on the planet.

There is nothing more violent than politics. Soldiers fight only when they are at war, but politics is a forever war. A politician's most dangerous enemies are almost always hiding in the ranks of their own army, and the speed at which everything occurs further reduces the margin of error and increases the mortality rate. In this milieu, intellectuals are generally useless because they never put their hand to their sword hilt—a fatal mistake in a game where risk-taking is the only real currency.

Ultimately, it is a leap in the dark. I will always remember John Podesta, an advisor to both Clinton and Obama—an edgy, wired, wiry man who looked like he did too much jogging—addressing a young mayor of Florence and his scribe during one of our pilgrimages to the heart of the empire. We had been asking him about choosing the right moment to launch a national campaign. 'You don't wait for the right moment to do it,' he told us. 'You do it and you hope that it'll be the right moment.' That advice brought us luck, for a while.

Borgians are organisms particularly well adapted to periods of turbulence, when a political system is confronted with its own finite nature, when the only good responses to uncertainty are the same as those to danger: speed and force. The hour of the predator is essentially just a return to normality. The anomaly was the brief period during which we believed that we could curb the bloody quest for power with a system of rules.

However shocking they are for us, the acts of the Borgians are simply an updated version of what is described in the history books, in Plutarch's *Lives* and Suetonius's *The Twelve Caesars*, in chronicles of the Renaissance and the *ancien régime*.

Today's Borgians do not read history books, but they know another Borgian when they see one. When MBS threw his torture party at the Ritz-Carlton, Trump—who was president at the time—wrote on Twitter: 'I have great confidence in King Salman and the Crown Prince of Saudi Arabia, they know exactly what they are doing… Some of those they are harshly treating have been "milking" their country for years!'

In this, the hour of the predator, it is no longer leaders in formerly peripheral states who are trying to resemble our leaders, but Western leaders adopting non-native traits. While Europe's ruling class may be disconcerted by the fact that the president of the United States is governing with a coterie of family members and business associates, that is not the case for autocrats, who find it perfectly natural to appeal to one of the president's friends or relatives to ask for favourable treatment. Inevitably, the same logic is now taking over Western governments, where opening a diplomatic channel with one of Trump's distant cousins or golf partners is what passes for statesmanship.

All that matters is the result. As Javier Milei put it so succinctly: 'What is the difference between a madman and a genius? Success!' This is the credo of the Borgians, now shared by a majority of the world's population, who have stopped regarding the rules as a guarantee of their freedom and started to see them as a gigantic swindle, if not an elite conspiracy, designed to oppress them.

'The first thing we do, let's kill all the lawyers,' said Shakespeare. Or, rather, Dick the Butcher in *Henry VI*, discussing how to spark an uprising against the government of the king of England. According to Dick, lawyers are the accomplices of the powers that be, men without morals, willing to support anything they are told to support. Lawyers do not solve problems, but create them, and they always have some loophole to hand. They care only about form, not substance, and the language they speak is deliberately unintelligible because they want to pull the wool over the eyes of the poor. At the end of the day, they are just looking after themselves.

Borgians focus on substance, not form. They promise to solve the people's real problems: crime, immigration, the cost of living. And how do their opponents respond, all those liberals and progressives and democrats? They respond with rules, democracy in peril, protection for minorities, et cetera.

Of all the Democrat presidential and vice-presidential candidates in the United States since 1980, Tim Walz— Kamala Harris's running mate—was the first not to have a law degree. Twenty candidates in ten elections, over a forty-year period: lawyers all the way down. In the same period, none of the four Republican presidents had a legal background: the first, Ronald Reagan, was an actor, while the three others were businessmen.

In the United States, lawyers are the second most-hated profession, just behind politicians. Is it really surprising, then, that the party of lawyers has been swept aside? That a platform entirely created by lawyers, based around the defence of democratic procedures and respect for minorities, whose principal argument consisted of legal challenges against the Republican candidate, lost out to the grievances of the Borgians: inflation, immigration, class resentment?

Lawyers have many qualities, but they have never managed to stop a revolution. In fact, it is their qualities that almost always make them the revolutionaries' first target. If there is one figure that attracts hate and rage during an insurrection, it is the man who refuses to join the mob, who raises not his fist but his finger to raise objections, to demand that procedures are followed. Worse still if he does it to defend an enemy of the people, a king that Dick the Butcher would rightly like to see lynched.

CHICAGO, NOVEMBER 2017

'THE WHITE HOUSE kitchen garden was symbolically powerful. Growing eggplant and zucchini and showing images of the First Lady kneeling in the dirt, surrounded by children, sent a very strong message to the nation and to the world.'

The main hall of the Chicago Science Museum is abuzz with excitement. We are here for the inaugural dinner of the foundation established by Barack Obama after leaving the White House.

A year has passed since the political earthquake that was Donald Trump's election victory. Europe is now facing the disastrous effects of Brexit. In Italy, the polls for the upcoming spring elections suggest an unprecedented wave of nationalist populism is heading our way.

We are here in search of... I won't say answers, but at least ideas. In recent years, despite his limitations, Obama has been a beacon of hope for liberal democrats all over the world. Even now, our instinctive reaction is to turn to him for advice. That's why we were so enthusiastic about his decision to create a foundation: at last, we have somewhere to think about what comes next, to protect ourselves from the reactionary tsunami that threatens to engulf the West.

We have travelled more than 4,000 miles to be here tonight. And now we are listening to the former White House chef tell us about the merits of Michelle's organic vegetable garden. After the chef, another speaker goes up on stage. His name is Michael Hebb. Checking his biography online, I discover that he pioneered the mindful consumption of chocolate in the workplace, before founding an organization called Death over Dinner.

Somewhat shaken by these opening speeches, I turn to the other guests. They are certainly interesting characters: 'leaders-in-waiting' whom the foundation intends to 'inspire and connect so that they can change the world'. The chef's organic broccoli is now being served. Our dining companions have just begun making small talk when a young woman seated at our table speaks up.

'Good evening, my name is Heather and I'll be your conversation facilitator tonight.' Following this brief introduction, we discover to our horror that the format for the dinner does not allow guests to interact spontaneously with one another. Instead, our conversation will be guided by Heather, who will enable us to move beyond the usual civilities and engage in a higher level of discussion. To this end, the guests are asked to take turns answering five questions: 'How did I get my name? Who are my family? Who was my biggest influence? Who would I like to be? How involved do I feel with my community?'

To break the ice, Heather gives us a brief and very engaging description of her life as a transgender immigrant, adopted by a family in Chicago. As I listen to her story, I wonder how anybody else is going to be able to follow this. Then, looking around at the other tables, I realize that the same exercise is being played out all over the room. Each table has its own conversation facilitator who is asking the dinner guests the same five questions.

From the corner of my eye, I glimpse the awkward expression on the face of Captain Rocca, the security guard who has accompanied us on this trip. As the evening wears on, I will see this muscular, jovial, courageous man, who would unhesitatingly take a bullet to protect us, visibly shrink until he is nothing more than a trembling twig.

After dinner is over, he sits at the bar with me, sipping a restorative Scotch, and tells me about his ordeal. After his initial shock, he managed to overcome his inhibitions and everything went reasonably well until the moment when he dared to reply 'Myself' to the question 'Who would you like to be?' At which point he was the victim of a pile-on from the other guests, who heaped insults on him, with even the conversation facilitator calling him out for his egotism.

We laughed about it that night, but I couldn't help thinking that, had he been an American voter, Captain Rocca—one of the few working-class people at that event—would have emerged from the Obama Foundation's inaugural dinner a fully fledged Trump supporter. And I suspect that none of the other activities planned for the thirty-six-hour symposium would change his mind: not the 7 a.m. meditation session (thankfully listed as 'optional' in the programme), nor the interview with Prince Harry on youth as a vector of social transformation, nor Michelle Obama's dialogue with a fashionable female poet on her sources of inspiration, nor even the private concert given by Gloria Estefan and the rapper Common—soberly rebranded as a 'community event'—that concluded the evening.

Two days later, we left Chicago with the feeling that we had met lots of nice, well-intentioned people who were singularly ill equipped to fight the coming battle.

Obama was a lawyer too. But, like Bill Clinton before him, his charisma and his political intelligence enabled him for a long time to avoid the pitfalls of his profession. After his second term was over, though, all that remained was a party of legal experts. Having given up the idea of transforming (or even regulating) capitalism, having given up fighting against economic inequality, the Democrats fell back on the less ambitious objective of representing minorities. Which is commendable in itself, but does nothing to challenge the dynamics that have moulded the entirety of American society since the early 1980s.

To make up for their lack of courage when it comes to the crucial issues, the lawyers went on an increasingly extremist crusade for minority rights, which led them to adopt positions way to the left of most of their own supporters. During her 2020 primary campaign, Kamala Harris talked about abolishing ICE (Immigration and Customs Enforcement), while also advocating public funding of sex-change operations for prisoners and illegal immigrants.

Not only did these positions prove ineffective with primary voters, but they came back to haunt the candidate four years later. One of the most striking ads in Trump's 2024 campaign played on non-binary pronouns: 'Harris is for they/them; Trump is for you.'

★

For the Borgians, wokeism has been a godsend: the perfect fuel for their chaos machine. Like the Ancient Greeks, who in a civil war would abolish civic rights for any citizens who did not take up arms for one side or the other—and like Dante, who sent them to the gates of hell to be tormented by wasps—the Borgians are most fearful of the undecided, those who refuse to pick a camp. So their objectives are served by anything that intensifies conflict.

No one understood this better than Alexander Nix, the former CEO of Cambridge Analytica. Around the time of our trip to Chicago, he can be found in an upstairs room of the Carlton Club, where I imagine him surrounded by men in vicuña suits, sipping Pol Roger as he pitches his company.

'We're not a run-of-the-mill communications agency,' he might say to these potential clients. 'If you want to sell Coke at a cinema and you ask a traditional agency, do you know what they'll say?'

Surprised by this unusual intro, the Thai billionaires, Kazakh oil executives and Argentine *estancieros* lean closer towards this elegantly dressed man, the most recent incarnation of a British lineage of empire-building privateers that can trace its roots back to the sixteenth century. Over the centuries, these pirates have turned from the high seas to private security firms and intelligence agencies, high finance and lobbying groups, but they are still the same men. They all have cut-glass accents, acquired in the costliest private schools, and they all wear three-piece tweed suits and leather shoes, never too new, because they want to project a certain air of nonchalance, testament to their flair for enjoying all the pleasures and privileges of life that they see as their right. They have the manners of an aristocrat and the moral code of a mob boss.

'Let me tell you what will happen if you go to see a traditional communications agency,' says the smooth-talking Nix of my imagination. 'They'll tell you: increase the points of sale, put a poster up in the entrance hall and a cardboard cut-out of a sexy girl drinking Coke near the till, and show an ad before the film starts. Just a load of useless ideas that won't sell a single extra can, but that will fund a whole economy of parasites, editors, photographers, video makers and creative directors who buy black T-shirts at Loro Piana and chug thirty-quid cocktails in Chelsea bars. We don't work like that. We're not interested in the Coke. What interests us is the customer. And do you know why the customer will buy a Coke? Not because it's cool, not because models drink it, not because of the forty-second ad that was more expensive to shoot than a Hollywood film. No, the customer will drink a Coca-Cola because he's thirsty. So, you want to know the only thing you need to do? Turn up the temperature in the cinema. That's what we do. We turn up the temperature. To make people thirsty. Simple, right?'

Cambridge Analytica closed its doors during the scandals that arose in the wake of the Brexit vote, but the online platforms where a part of our public life plays out follow exactly the same principle: they turn up the temperature to increase engagement. If the mobilization of prejudices has always been the lifeblood of political combat, social media has enabled it on an industrial scale. The principle is always the same. Three simple operations: identify the hot topics, the fracture points that divide public opinion; push the most extreme positions on these topics and get them in conflict with each other; get this conflict before as many eyeballs as possible, until the atmosphere grows overheated.

These platforms present themselves as a transparent window through which we can see the world as it is, free from the agendas of the elites that control traditional media. But they are more like fairground mirrors, distorting reality until it becomes unrecognizable, until it confirms all our expectations and biases.

Silicon Valley engineers long ago stopped programming computers and became instead programmers of human behaviour. From the moment when we decided to make social media the global interface of our relationship with reality, we put ourselves in their hands. And in the hands of everyone, from influencers to spin doctors, whose interest is served by the overheating of the social climate.

During the 2022 presidential elections in France, the far-right candidate Éric Zemmour made a telling Freudian slip. Intending to say: 'I only believe what I see,' he actually said: 'I only see what I believe.' But his gaffe merely confirmed the underlying logic of our age. And it would be a mistake to think we are immune to this, that it only applies to the others—to those who don't think the way we do—when in fact we are all subject to it, including the elites, who are no less vulnerable to manipulation and panic attacks than the angry masses.

MONTREAL, SEPTEMBER 2024

J USTIN TRUDEAU has a flair for finding the right setting. The room that he has chosen for his lunch meeting on artificial intelligence is on the tenth floor of a tower in the port of Montreal. The guests look out at the red-brick buildings in the old town and at the skyscrapers in the city centre before letting their gaze sweep across the St Lawrence River, gleaming majestically in the early-autumn sunlight.

In the absence of an official conversation facilitator, the guests chat spontaneously, intoxicated by the view more than by the bottle of Quebec Chardonnay from which they serve themselves sparingly. One man stands slightly apart from the rest, the thick-rimmed glasses that he wears giving him the look of someone whose gaze is turned inwards rather than outwards.

At a discreet nod from the Canadian prime minister, we take our seats around the table. Trudeau likes to present his country, not without reason, as the epicentre of 'responsible' AI. It's true that it was in Toronto that Geoffrey Hinton, winner of the Nobel Prize for Physics in 2024, led his research on artificial neural networks, while his colleague Yoshua Bengio continues to teach at the University of Montreal. Both men are characterized by an ethical concern that has become rare in our era, Hinton having quit Google, where he was employed as a consultant, so that he could express himself more freely on the risks of AI, and Bengio having turned down millions of dollars from all the major AI firms in order to preserve his independence.

Now, Yoshua Bengio is sitting across from his colleague Yann LeCun, who runs the AI laboratory at Meta, the group that owns Facebook, WhatsApp and Instagram. Since they jointly received the Turing Award for their work on deep learning in 2018, these three men—Hilton, Bengio and LeCun—have been considered the godfathers of 'artificial intelligence' as we know it today. The only problem: they agree on practically nothing. Which is somewhat annoying, since the entire planet is expecting them to shed light on a technological revolution that some already consider one of the great milestones in human history.

Their postures could hardly be more different. Bengio looks like a normal human being; his eyes don't have that glacial gleam shared by most of the tech conquistadors. Of all the experts in the field, he strikes me as the most credible. His judgements, his doubts, the sometimes disturbing questions he asks, are those of a scientist who is seeking to understand. When the greatest experts on a particular subject have such divergent views, he says, and make such discordant predictions, ranging from utopia to the destruction of the human species, it would seem wise for governing bodies to examine all the hypotheses rather than just choosing one of them.

Sitting across from him, Yann LeCun possesses a personality far more suited to the present time. His peremptory tone, free of any doubt or nuance, has made him very popular on X, where—at the time of writing—he has over 900,000 followers, compared to 18,000 for Bengio. Since taking over the AI division at Meta and being given the task of catching up with Google, LeCun has invested Zuckerberg's billions in open-source models that put the most powerful technology in human history in the hands of everyone, including the most extremist groups: a technology that, among its many amazing abilities, can provide each individual with a destructive power previously only available to countries. While other people worry about the uncontrolled spread of weapons of mass destruction, LeCun is unhesitating: artificial intelligence does not pose the slightest risk, and anyone who claims or imagines that it does must be a halfwit, including his former colleagues.

Sitting in this glass capsule suspended 200 feet above the ground, like a set from a science-fiction film, LeCun—with his thick glasses and his smug smile—reminds me of an Austin Powers who has grown a lot less amusing·with age. He starts out by telling us that we Europeans in the room are not able to buy the thick glasses he's wearing. Meta has decided not to sell them in Europe because of the EU's overly restrictive regulations. The big tech platforms always use this sort of blackmail: let us do what we want or you'll be left behind, relegated to the forgotten pages of history.

In reality, LeCun's connected glasses *are* available in Europe, where they are just as popular as they are everywhere else in the world. The ability for the wearer to transmit everything they see live on Facebook and Instagram has massive appeal for social media addicts. The only thing missing from the European model is one critical element: the system that allows the wearer to ask questions about what they're seeing and to obtain answers from Meta's artificial intelligence, in the process feeding it with a constant flow of new data.

LeCun has great expectations for his glasses. 'Ten years from now, there won't be any smartphones,' he declares. 'Only augmented reality glasses, okay? The computer will still be in our pocket, but we'll talk to our glasses. They'll display content that's superimposed on the real world.'

I only see what I believe. Thanks to Meta, the idea of seeing the world through rose-tinted (or any other colour) glasses is no longer a metaphor, but a part of our everyday lives. Everyone who wears them will be granted their own version of reality. Soon, ten people watching the same concert will have ten radically different experiences, with their augmented-reality glasses enabling them to add lighting effects, commercials, even guest artists. The same will be true for a business meeting, a political rally or a simple walk down the street.

Connected glasses fling open the gates to an enchanted kingdom. Imagine you're in a foreign country where you don't speak the language. You see a road sign: it's automatically translated and displayed in the field of vision of your augmented-reality glasses. You speak to someone and that person doesn't understand your language: the translation will be displayed in her glasses, and when she replies, the translation will be displayed in yours. You cross the street and your glasses warn you about the presence of a car you hadn't seen coming.

'There'll be lots of things like that,' says LeCun excitedly. 'After a while, your virtual assistant will know everything you're doing and will have a very precise idea of what you want. He'll even be able to predict what you might want next.'

And here, you see, is the endgame. Under the control of the tech oligarchs, the method we have chosen to interface with the world is jumping out of our pockets and becoming one with us, so that it can grant our wishes before we've even had time to think of them.

As the St Lawrence River sparkles on the horizon like a gigantic silicon chip, something dark flashes before my eyes. I don't need LeCun's glasses to see it. It's an image that is haunting me. The bleak image of a Chinese megacity, and of a billboard standing by the side of the Wuhan motorway, proclaiming in large letters: 'We create the future humanity dreams of.'

PARIS, SEPTEMBER 1931

T HE BEST RELATIONSHIP you can have with a mon-
arch is to be in a state of slight disgrace. As he walks
along the quays of the Île Saint-Louis, it is possible that
Curzio Malaparte is reflecting on these words of Admiral
von Tirpitz, which have always struck me as very wise.
Then again, maybe he sees things differently. The slight
disgrace into which he has fallen with Mussolini has cost
him his job at *La Stampa*, the prestigious Turin newspaper, where he had, at thirty, been its youngest ever editor.
This was a devastating blow for Malaparte, an ambitious
and committed fascist who had finally reached a position
where he was able to exercise political power and social
influence. On the other hand, since his disgrace was only
slight, it has not landed him in prison (where he will find
himself two years later), but simply on the banks of the

Seine, where he is free to enjoy his books and society dinner parties.

This is not the first time Malaparte has found himself sidelined. You might almost say that this tendency to be out of step with the wider world is an integral part of his personality. Born in Tuscany, Kurt Erich Suckert had a father who was not only German but an anxious, authoritarian Protestant, plus a mother who didn't love him. At fifteen, he ran away from home to join the French army so he could fight against the Germans in the First World War. After the war, he joined the fascist party in Italy before it even took power, writing inflammatory articles for several periodicals. But his best friend was Piero Gobetti, the youngest and most brilliant of Italy's anti-fascist intellectuals, and as soon as he was made editor of *La Stampa*, Malaparte fired the newspaper's party-approved hacks and hired the best young writers of his generation: Corrado Alvaro, Elio Vittorini, Alberto Moravia.

His relationship with Mussolini mirrored his zigzagging affiliations: Il Duce appreciated his talents, but didn't trust him. Mussolini knew that this was someone totally unpredictable, someone who would throw his best friend under a train for a perfectly turned phrase. So he threw him under the train first.

And so, in the summer of 1931, Malaparte's slight disgrace leads to his exile in France. But he is not in Paris only to stroll along the quays, talk politics and literature with his writer friends Daniel Halévy and Jean Guéhenno, or revel in the splendour of Princess Bibesco's salons, however much he enjoys all these activities. He has just published a short tract on the *Technique of the Coup d'État*. In this book, Malaparte analyses the method used by both far-right and far-left parties who reject liberal democracy and 'place the problem of the state in revolutionary territory'.

Malaparte's knowledge of such movements is not theoretical; he has seen them at work. As a very young man, he took part in the Supreme War Council at Versailles. Next, attached to the Italian legation in Poland, he witnessed the confrontation between Marshal Piłsudski and the Bolshevik army. Back in Italy, he was a participant in the March on Rome and Mussolini's rise to power. As a journalist, he travelled to the USSR, providing some of the most enlightening reports on the internal struggles of the new Soviet regime in the late 1920s.

The idea he drew from all of this, and which he then presented in *Technique of the Coup d'État*, is also revolutionary: something has changed, Malaparte remarked, in the way that power is seized, even though most people, including liberal and democratic leaders, don't realize it. Revolution has become less a political event and more a technical problem, with the result that a thousand well-organized men have more chance of seizing control of the state than an armed revolutionary mob.

To illustrate his argument, Malaparte highlights the critical example of the October Revolution. Alexander Kerensky, who took control of Russia following the tsar's abdication, was far from weak or incapable, according to Malaparte. He showed determination and courage, first in putting down an uprising of workers and deserters, then the reactionary revolt led by General Kornilov. In the autumn of 1917, he took every possible precaution against a possible Bolshevik insurrection. The same precautions that any leader of a liberal government would take, Malaparte adds sadistically, naming them one by one: Poincaré, Lloyd George, MacDonald, Giolitti, Stresemann. Aware of the risk of a violent coup, Kerensky took care to defend the bureaucratic and political organs of the state: the Winter Palace, the ministries, the parliament building, the general staff. Exactly what any sensible head of state would have done.

Except that he was pitted against a man who had understood that the rules of the game had changed. Trotsky's stance was that the revolutionaries must ignore the existence of Kerensky's government. The key to the state was not its bureaucratic and political organs—it wasn't the Tauride Palace or the Mariinsky Palace or the Winter Palace—but the technical infrastructure: the power stations, the railways, the telephone and telegraph systems, the ports, the gas holders, the aqueducts.

'To seize control of the modern state,' said Trotsky (or at least Malaparte's version of Trotsky), 'you need troops and technicians: teams of armed men led by engineers.'

His own comrades in the party were doubtful about this; their idea had always been for a mass insurrection—the proletarian revolution—not a surgical operation led by a handful of specialists.

But Trotsky, unfazed, pursued his plan. In the chaos that reigned around Petrograd, nobody noticed the small groups of unarmed workers and sailors moving through the corridors of the telephone and telegraph exchanges and the post offices, nor the technicians examining the layout of gas and water pipes, electricity cables, telephone and telegraph wires. And whenever they passed in the corridors or stairways of these offices, Trotsky's agents pretended not to know one another.

On 21 October, the teams given the task of taking control of the train stations went through a full dress rehearsal. It was a complete success. Nobody noticed them. The same day, Malaparte wrote, three sailors went to the power station near the entrance of the port. The manager greeted them enthusiastically: 'At last!' he said. 'It's been weeks since I asked the military command to send me someone to protect the station.' The three Bolsheviks moved into the power station—to defend it against Red Guards, they said, in the event of an uprising. Other sailors took control of other municipal power stations following the same playbook.

On 24 October, Trotsky launched the attack. It all happened in a few hours. The technicians of the Red Army seized the nerve centres of the state without touching the political centres: the parliament, the ministries, the government headquarters all remained in place. This was the first time, wrote Malaparte, that we have seen an insurrection proclaim victory while leaving the hands of government free. Lenin himself was unconvinced. The next day, he went to the Smolny Palace to attend the Second Soviet Congress disguised as a worker, his beard shaved and wearing a wig. When Trotsky spotted him, he said mockingly: 'Why are you in disguise? The victors don't have to hide.'

'ELON, I'VE INITIATED a policy debate inspired by ideas from you and Milei. While migration control is crucial for Germany, the AfD stands against freedom, business—and it's a far-right extremist party. Don't rush to conclusions from afar. Let's meet, and I'll show you what the FDP stands for.'

Among the hundreds of thousands of messages posted daily on social media by politicians from all over the world, it is difficult to find one that is more pathetic, more simple-minded, more desperately naïve than this post from Christian Lindner, the former finance minister and leader of Germany's liberal democrat party, sent on 20 December 2024 to Elon Musk.

The response of the world's richest man was not long in coming. 'The traditional political parties in Germany have utterly failed the people. AfD is the only hope for Germany.'

After backing Bolsonaro and Milei in South America, and Bukele in Central America, and after making a massive contribution to Trump's election victory in the United States, Musk has turned his sights on Europe. In Britain, he has offered his support to Reform UK, the party behind Brexit, and in Germany to the AfD, the party of the extreme right.

Anyone who imagines that such behaviour is just another show of eccentricity from the South African billionaire would be making a fatal mistake. In fact, Musk's approach reveals something much more fundamental, something that goes far beyond the political preferences of one man, however powerful he may be. This is something with much deeper roots and it is destined to have far graver consequences.

The tech conquistadors have decided to get rid of the old political elites. If they get their way, the world of Lindner and all his kind—the liberals and the social democrats, the conservatives and the progressives: everything we have grown used to considering as the cornerstone of our democracies—will be swept away.

Until now, the economic elites—the financiers, entre-preneurs and CEOs—have relied on a political class of technocrats (or would-be technocrats) from the right and the left: moderate, boring, all more or less the same. These technocrats governed their countries on the basis of liberal democratic principles and in accordance with the rules of the market, sometimes tempered by social considerations.

This was the Davos consensus. A place where blue ski slopes, softly marked out by snowploughs, have replaced the wild convulsions of Thomas Mann's *The Magic Mountain*.

In the hour of the predator, this equilibrium has been blown to pieces. The new technological elites—the Musks and the Zuckerbergs—have nothing in common with the technocrats of Davos. Their philosophy of life is not founded on competent management of the status quo, but rather on an urge to disrupt and cause havoc. Order, prudence, respect for the rules: such ideas are anathema to these men who have made their fortunes by moving fast and breaking things, to quote Facebook's original internal motto.

The overlords of tech have far more in common with the Borgians. Like the Borgians, they are almost invaria-bly outliers and outsiders who have had to break rules to achieve success. Like the Borgians, they are suspicious of experts and elites, of all those who represent the old guard and who might prevent them pursuing their dreams. Like the Borgians, they are men of action who believe they can mould reality to their own desires. Like the Borgians, they live in a world where profit trumps truth and where speed serves the strongest. Like the Borgians, they feel nothing but contempt for the politicians and the bureaucrats, seeing them as weak hypocrites whose time has come and gone. Thanks to the internet and social media, the weakness and hypocrisy of these former elites has been exposed to the eyes of the whole world.

In reality, the overlords of tech *are* Borgians—and this convergence goes far beyond the role, however important, that any of their individual representatives might play.

From this point of view, the re-election of Trump also marks a tipping point because now, for the first time, the tech conquistadors feel powerful enough to declare war on the old elites. Until this moment, the convergence between the Borgians and the tech leaders was hidden by the fact that the latter didn't dare openly contest the supremacy of the Davos bloc. For many years, the over-lords of tech have had to advance through stealth and diplomacy, to be foxes rather than lions, even if, deep inside, they yearned to roar their superiority over the chiefs of the old political tribes.

Before Musk, there was Eric Schmidt.

Based on his education, character and tactical calculations, Eric Schmidt is the polar opposite of Elon Musk. Where the latter is shameless and transgressive, the former is quiet, discreet, conciliatory. To see him wander through the corridors of the Pentagon or shake hands with the optimates of the Aspen Institute, looking a little gauche in his overlarge suit, ever-smiling, an expression of infinite tolerance on his face, you might mistake him for a country vicar, a pillar of his community. In truth, he is more like a cardinal, one of those cunning men too aware of their own power to want to sit in the Chair of St Peter.

The father of Charles VIII was determined that the Dauphin should not learn more Latin than these five words: *Qui nescit dissimulare, nescit regnare*—'He who cannot dissemble, cannot rule'. While Eric Schmidt's father was not the king of France, but simply a professor of international economics, he must have taught his son a similar lesson.

At the start of the twenty-first century, when Google was heading for disaster and the two brilliant sociopaths who had founded it realized that they needed an adult in the room, they hired Eric Schmidt. From that moment on, Schmidt took control of the company, turning Google into the behemoth it is today and leaving Larry and Sergey, the two founders, free to devote themselves to the post-human pursuits that actually interested them. During board meetings at Mountain View, the two of them would typically remain glued to their screens until Schmidt cleared his throat and announced: 'Larry, Sergey, I need your attention on this point.' Then they would resurface for a few moments before returning to their metaphysical quest.

During the Obama presidency, Schmidt was omnipresent. Whenever there was an issue involving science, technology, computing or industrial policy, he would appear, smiling beatifically in his baggy suit, as if ready at a moment's notice to make the sign of the cross and bless the members of his audience.

In 2012, his contribution to the re-election of the Democrat president was far more important than Musk's contribution to Trump's 2024 victory. Back then, things weren't looking good for Obama. The enthusiasm surrounding his election had long ago died down, the economy was taking a long time to recover, and American soldiers continued to be killed by 'improvised explosive devices' in Iraq and Afghanistan. Of all the ingredients that had enabled his electoral triumph, there was only one still worth betting on: the internet. Thankfully, His Eminence Eric Schmidt was on hand to help.

On 20 January 2011, the White House announced its team for the president's re-election campaign. Jim Messina, who had been in charge of the digital part of the previous campaign, was now given the lead role. On the same day, at Mountain View, Eric Schmidt discreetly resigned from his duties as Google's CEO, remaining only as executive chairman, a role that would leave his hands free to help his protégé Messina with the task of re-electing their good friend Barack. Together, the two men developed their strategy: to build the biggest electoral database ever seen, with the aim of individually targeting every voter in every state. If the 2008 campaign was the one that used the internet as a communication tool, the 2012 campaign used it as an information tool.

The operation was codenamed Project Narwhal, in tribute to the long-horned cetacean that surges up monstrously from the depths to shock its rivals. The Republicans wouldn't see it coming. For months, six days a week and fourteen hours a day, dozens of engineers lent to the campaign by Google—but also by Twitter, Facebook and several other Silicon Valley companies—worked to create this powerful beast of the sea. Thanks to Project Narwhal, Obama began his re-election year with the certainty that he knew the name of all 69,456,897 Americans whose votes had carried him to the White House. Of course, these votes had been cast secretly, but

Narwhal's data was so detailed that the analysts were able to identify the Obama supporters in every district. Each elector was given a probability rating between zero and a hundred. Zero meant they would vote for Romney. A hundred meant they were a guaranteed Obama supporter. The trick was to ignore those voters and focus all the campaign's resources on voters in swing states with scores between forty-five and fifty-five.

Throughout the campaign, Narwhal tracked these 'useful' voters house by house, sending each a message adapted to their ideas and interests. Having seen the grand vision of 2008 crash into the wall of reality, Obama's strategists reversed course. From a mobilization tool, the internet was transformed into a segmentation tool. This was child's play for Schmidt, as the leader of the biggest advertising company on the planet, but it constituted a revolution in American and global politics. In 2012, for the first time, the electoral campaign of the world's leading democracy became a software war. And, thanks to the cardinal of tech, the Democrats' machine proved effortlessly superior.

On election night, Schmidt was at the campaign headquarters in Chicago. A blurry photograph shows him in a check shirt and jeans, surrounded by people eating French fries. That night, Obama won only 51 per cent of the vote—three and a half million fewer votes than in the previous election—but strategically targeted in a way that enabled him to capture the vast majority of electoral college votes. If the 2008 victory had been political, the 2012 victory was essentially technical.

From that day on, the tech cardinal's aura of sanctity permeated every corner of the Democratic administration. Two weeks after Obama's re-election, the anti-trust committee, which had started legal action against Google, closed the case. Already a member of the White House Office of Science and Technology, Schmidt was appointed chairman of the Defense Innovation Board, the office in charge of strategies to 'ensure U.S. technological and military dominance', in the words of the mission statement that Schmidt himself wrote for this new organization. He was also named head of the first committee on artificial intelligence. The cardinal was now at the centre of power, and his word was the last word when it came to every aspect of the future.

The story of the Google cardinal is only the most flagrant example among the numerous cases of tech conquistadors working closely with the Democrats. This went on for years. Until the Biden presidency, in fact.

Because of this cosy relationship, the party of lawyers, usually so punctilious when it came to enforcing standards and laws, somehow forgot to impose any rules at all on the platforms where a large part of the nation's political life was being played out. Even after Trump's first election victory, when it became clear that the power of the platforms was profoundly altering the way American democracy worked, the Democrats never seriously attempted to impose any real responsibility on those who had become the new masters of politics. And when the game shifted onto the terrain of artificial intelligence, the party of lawyers maintained its impassive indifference, contenting itself with a few cordial conversations with the bosses of Google and Microsoft. It is because of this that, instead of developing under the guidance of government—as was the case for atomic weapons and other military technologies—AI has escaped all regulatory control and is in the hands of private companies that have elevated themselves to the ranks of nation states.

For thirty years, from the mid 1990s to the present day, American Democrats have been bowing down to the tech entrepreneurs, enabling them to transform themselves from easy-going nerds with a hint of autism, promoting a future of universal brotherhood, into terrifying aliens, still with a hint of autism, engaged in a merciless war for planetary and intergalactic supremacy.

'In some senses, the Mexican empire was conquered by the Mexicans,' noted one of the first historians of the Spanish takeover at the time of Moctezuma II. A handful of adventurers, without maps or any knowledge of the local language or customs, could never possibly have seized control of the most powerful state in the Americas, and its capital city of 200,000 inhabitants, had it not been able to rely on the complicity of local chiefs, intimidated by the newcomers' magic or tantalized by the lure of personal advancement.

In our age of digital colonization, moderate leaders performed the same function. Some of them went even further, joining the ranks of the new conquistadors. Take the former vice-president Al Gore, for example, who—after directing the White House's internet policy—made hundreds of millions of dollars, first at Apple and then at a venture capital company in Silicon Valley. Or take Nick Clegg, the former British deputy prime minister, who became Mark Zuckerberg's lobbyist-in-chief before being dismissed, like the mere underling that he always was, a few days after Trump's re-election.

Because, in the meantime, as might have been expected, the conquistadors have let their masks fall. Nobody doubts the sincerity of figures such as Eric Schmidt and Bill Gates, who presented themselves as progressive Democrats. And some among the tech leaders still consider themselves as such. But what's clear now is that, beyond their individual preferences, the convergence between the overlords of tech and the Borgians is structural. These two species of predators both draw their power from the digital revolution, and they cannot tolerate any limits to its will to power: the lawyers are their natural enemies, the prey that must be devoured to allow this new world to flourish.

In the hour of the predator, Borgians all over the planet are offering up the territories that they govern like a mass laboratory to the digital conquistadors, so that they can develop their vision of the future there, without being encumbered by laws or rights from another age. MBS is building enclaves where the only laws will be the laws of technology; Bukele has adopted bitcoin as his country's official currency; Milei plans to construct nuclear power stations to supply AI servers. For his part, Trump has given over entire swathes of his administration to the hottest heads from the Valley. Under their leadership, the world is being transformed into a patchwork of territories charging headlong towards a post-human future, with no guardrails whatsoever.

The lawyers bowed down to the new masters, not only in the United States but all over the world. They thought their submission would save them, but of course it doesn't work like that. Even now that the sky has come crashing down, most of them still don't understand what has happened, as illustrated perfectly by that cringe-worthy tweet from the leader of the German liberals. They still think that a break-up of the Musk-Trump alliance could be a game-changer. You get the feeling that they will continue thinking like this until someone bursts the bubble of their delusion, as the conservative philosopher Joseph de Maistre did to a French aristocrat, the Marquise de Costa, several years after the 1789 Revolution: 'Madame, we must have the courage to admit it: for a long time we have failed to understand the revolution that we witnessed; for a long time we had thought of it as an *event*. We were wrong: it is an *epoch*.'

ROME, OCTOBER 1998

OLD AGE IS ALWAYS portrayed as the apogee of wisdom. But it's a beautiful thing when it turns into the exact opposite. There is nothing more irresistible than the madness of an old man who has rid himself of all his complexes and ambitions, who no longer has any need or desire to please others, and who tells it like it is, smiling with pleasure as he tries to scare his listeners, and sometimes even succeeds.

When I was twenty, I used to know a man like that. He'd read my first book and would invite me to lunch from time to time. He liked having someone who would listen to his stories. His name was Francesco Cossiga, and he was famously intelligent and famously depressed. He'd been Italy's minister of the interior at the time when Aldo

Moro was kidnapped, then prime minister and president of the Italian Republic. None of these positions calmed his bipolar nature, and his moments of exaltation alternated with periods of despondency. When I met him, he seemed like the kind of man who woke up in the morning worrying about how he was going to fill the day. And he focused the Machiavellian intelligence that had led him to the summit of Italian politics, through some of the darkest hours in the Years of Lead, on one single aim: to have fun, if possible while making his friends smile and his numerous enemies shudder with fear. He told tall tales, analysed the present situation, lifted the curtain on public life, and now and then gave an interview that would send shockwaves through the world of Roman politics. These interviews were little monuments of political intelligence, cynicism, fierce and indifferent irony.

At night, he would watch TV shopping shows on local channels. Then he would call the switchboard and order a complete set of knives. 'I-am Fran-ces-co Cos-si-ga,' he would say in his Sardinian accent, enunciating every syllable with Teutonic precision. The switchboard operators, amazed, would send him the knives for free.

He was fascinated by espionage and technology. One day, after lunch, he sat on the sofa and began typing into his mobile phone. I thought he was making a call, but after a few minutes he was still staring with intense concentration at his phone, tapping away at the keyboard. I started to fear that he was really losing it this time. In fact, he was sending one of the first texts ever sent in Italy. At the time, nobody imagined that the telephone would become a means for exchanging written messages. Only the former president and the head of the intelligence services sent each other texts in those days.

And then, one day, he emerged from his torpor and he brought down the Prodi government. I was working for that government at the time, filled with all the passion of a young idealist. I didn't see him for a while after that: he no longer struck me as quite so amusing. Then, one day, I bumped into him on the square in front of the Pantheon, surrounded by the same little crowd of courtiers that always gathers around the powerful in Rome.

'President, what happened…?'

He looked at me as if he'd never seen me before. And then he made a gesture, as if to say that it was all the same thing: the fall of the government, the texts, the knives from those late-night shopping shows.

Later he explained that he'd had no choice: the United States had decided to bomb Kosovo, and the far left, which supported Prodi, would not allow Italian military bases to be used by the Americans. 'The problem with the Americans,' he said, 'is that they live in a world of yes and no, and they're not familiar with the typical turns of phrase in the language of Italian politics like "maybe" or "however".'

Cossiga's realpolitik was responsible for one of the first political disappointments of my life. But I have to admit that, even after this, I continued to have a soft spot for old people still capable of achieving the unexpected. This is the spirit of Tolstoy who, at eighty-two, absconded from home and died at a railway station, waiting for a train to who-knows-where. It is the spirit of the elderly Sartre, who renounced Marxism and began studying the Torah, scandalizing the champagne communists of the Left Bank. (Betraying one's disciples: another of the little-known benefits of senility...) It is the spirit of everyone who prefers to continue setting a bad example rather than boring their progeny with sensible advice.

On the face of it, Henry Kissinger does not fit this pattern; he was more like an anatomist of power who continued cultivating his networks until the end. He even celebrated his hundredth birthday four times—in New York, in Connecticut, in the English countryside and in Bavaria—so as not to let down any of his countless acolytes.

A former advisor to JFK, then secretary of state under Richard Nixon, plus a historian and diplomat, Kissinger was the last representative of the generation marked by the Second World War who had access to all the leaders of this world; the last wise old man who could fly off to Beijing to have a conversation with Xi Jinping, then deliver a confidential message to the president of the United States.

He was intimately familiar with all the pleasures and frustrations of being an advisor. It is, he said, 'like sitting next to a driver who's heading toward the edge of a cliff and asking you to check that the gas tank is full and the tyre pressure is good'.

Beyond a penchant for realpolitik, the other quality that Kissinger shared with his friend Cossiga was a savage sense of humour. When you're in politics, he said, you have only two choices: either you're intentionally funny or you're unintentionally funny. So it's better to make people laugh on purpose.

When he was asked how to prepare to play a role in world politics, Kissinger would quote Winston Churchill: 'Study history, study history. In history lies all the secrets of statecraft.' This is the height of transgression in an age when the Borgians are betting on our fading memories to rewrite history and reopen the wounds that festered into the anti-democratic movements of the first half of the twentieth century, while the tech overlords use their ignorance of the past as a marketing strategy.

'It's great to be back in Beijing! I kicked off my visit with a run through Tiananmen Square,' wrote Mark Zuckerberg in a 2016 Facebook post accompanied by a photograph of him in shorts, jogging across the square where the Chinese army massacred protesting students in 1989. 'I have learned to use the word "impossible" with great caution. And I hope you guys take that attitude about your lives,' boasted Jeff Bezos, citing a Nazi scientist as the inspiration for his space expedition.

Having said that, Kissinger was the opposite of nostalgic. He was driven by curiosity, by a desire to understand—a desire so sadly lacking in the current generation of powerful men. For those who know how to use it, history is above all a means of understanding what is truly new.

Kissinger once talked about being at a conference in 2015. He had planned to skip the session on artificial intelligence, a subject about which he knew nothing and which he imagined did not concern him in the slightest. But some Germanic scruple made him attend the meeting anyway. There, to his stupefaction, he heard Demis Hassabis, the creator of DeepMind, introducing a software that could defeat the world champion at

Go, generally considered the most complex game ever invented. Kissinger understood instantly that something much greater was at stake here. And that, in contrast to what he'd imagined, this was something that did concern him, as a 'historian and part-time statesman'.

In a 2018 article for *The Atlantic* about artificial intelligence, he wrote: 'Human cognition loses its personal character. Individuals turn into data, and data become regnant.' AI was not simply an accelerator of power; it was a new form of power, distinguishing it from all the machines invented by humans before it. Where automation dealt with means, AI dealt with ends: it developed its own objectives. 'Through this process, artificial intelligence develops an ability previously thought to be reserved for human beings. It makes strategic judgments about the future.'

Where his younger colleagues—Democrat lawyers or Davos optimates—saw only a technical development, Kissinger realized that the dawn of AI was also a political development. As, I think, would my late friend Cossiga, or any of the brilliant leaders of his generation. Having experienced warfare in their youth, none of them would have fallen into the trap of imagining power as a competition between technocrats armed with PowerPoint slides. They may not have read the works of the French theologian François Fénelon, but they instinctively knew that humans cannot hope that a superior power will remain within the bounds of moderation. With their passing, we have lost this wisdom just at the moment when a new superior power is making its appearance. As an anatomist of power, Kissinger was able to perceive its deepest nature. The way he described it, AI was a Borgian technology, with its power residing in its capacity to produce shock and awe. Like the Borgians, AI feeds on chaos and turns it into surprise. Its capacity for action is still limited, of course, but the next generation of software, able to carry out tasks autonomously, is already on the horizon. Like the Borgians, AI does not care about rules or procedures. Nobody, not even its creators, knows how it comes to its decisions. All that matters is the result—'Success!' as Milei would say—with any and all means being justified by the desired ends. There is nothing democratic or transparent about the power of AI. Rather than artificial intelligence, AI is actually a form of *authoritarian* intelligence, centralizing data and transforming it into power. All of this in almost total obscurity, controlled by a handful of entrepreneurs and scientists, who are riding the tiger and hoping it doesn't eat them alive.

The great dilemma that structured twentieth-century politics was the relationship between the state and the market: what part of our life and the workings of our society should be under the control of the state, and what part should be left to the market and civil society? In the twenty-first century, the decisive rift is becoming that between humans and machines. To what extent should our lives be subject to powerful digital systems—and on what conditions? Ultimately, individuals and societies are going to have to decide which aspects of life belong to human intelligence and which aspects we can entrust to AI, or to a collaboration between humans and AI. And every time they choose the human option, when AI could guarantee more efficient results, there will be a price to pay.

WHAT STRIKES ME is the dismay among the audience. And yet all of us on stage have played our parts. The American president's scientific advisor has asked neutral, polite questions, with the aim of smoothing things over and, above all, not causing any disruption to the tech overlords' triumphal monologue.

Sam Altman, the CEO of OpenAI, has taken his turn speaking, his eyes wide open, giving him the permanently startled look of a woodland creature—a deer or a rabbit, perhaps—although this impression is contradicted by his monotone voice and the will to limitless power that seeps through every phrase he utters, even the most anodyne.

Demis Hassabis has embodied the smiling version of the post-human, rendered perhaps even more disturbing by his Mediterranean warmth, since we sense that he believes what he's saying, that for him it is not a question of money or power, that he truly thinks humanity's only hope is trust in the digital god that he is creating in the DeepMind laboratory.

As for me, I initially played one of my favourite parts: the guy whose presence on stage nobody can quite understand, and who, by all the laws of logic, shouldn't be here at all. And then the penny dropped. The organizers of this closed-door discussion on the future of AI needed a token human. Alongside the demigods busy dreaming up artificially enhanced tomorrows, they wanted a more-or-less normal human being who could express a few doubts about the whole enterprise. And it would be a particularly humiliating form of desertion to turn down the role of the human, I decided.

From my experience as an Aztec scribe, it's true that I am profoundly ignorant when it comes to artificial intelligence. On the other hand, my experience of politics has allowed me to develop a certain expertise when it comes to natural stupidity. And when we consider the future of artificial intelligence, we have to admit that it won't only amplify human intelligence—it will also amplify our stupidity.

So it is that I find myself, one spring afternoon, at a hotel in Lisbon, in front of a small cross section of Kissinger's legendary address book: the secretary-general and the military commander of NATO, the president of the European parliament, two or three heads of government, a host of ministers, commissioners and intelligence chiefs, a few assorted billionaires and the CEOs of several very large companies.

It's a conspiracy theorist's ultimate fantasy: a gathering of the Illuminati who are supposedly controlling the destiny of the world. And yet, had that conspiracy theorist attended this meeting with an open mind—an unlikely presupposition, I admit, for a conspiracy theorist—he would have witnessed a curious phenomenon.

As Altman and Hassabis spoke that evening, the faces in the audience looked increasingly discomfited. Since the former appears to be on the spectrum and the latter completely absorbed by his messianic quest, the heads of OpenAI and DeepMind were blithely unaware of what was happening around them, but the phenomenon was striking nonetheless. As they listened to these two popes of AI, it gradually dawned on the simple mortals in the audience—even if they were among the most powerful mortals on the planet—that there was not the slightest point of contact between their experience of life and the new world that was being laid out before their eyes. And, even worse, that there was no possibility of establishing any human relationship with these bringers of the Good News because they were already inhabiting another world, where everything that has, until now, constituted the essence of the human adventure—the autonomy of the individual, for starters—has ceased to mean anything at all. And the more that these tech overlords attempted to put them at their ease, the more the audience members could feel an icy hand caressing their spine. At one point, watching them slump ever deeper into their seats, I remembered the look on poor Captain Rocca's face that night in Chicago, six years before. This afternoon in Lisbon, the faces of Kissinger's friends—these political leaders, these business leaders—wore precisely the same expression as Captain Rocca's had. It made no difference that they were so much higher up the food chain. It made no difference that there were hundreds of Captain Roccas posted around the building to guarantee their safety. It didn't matter how many helicopters and elite snipers were waiting in the shadows to keep Kissinger's friends out of harm's way. The truth was that the position in which they found themselves, in relation to AI, was exactly the same as that of every Captain Rocca in Lisbon and all over the rest of the planet. They were united by the same feeling of dismay.

When confronted with the brave new world presented to them, Kissinger's friends were just as lost as any other random human. Even more lost, perhaps, since their role obliged them to look further forward into the future, to make choices, develop plans, calculate investments. To this end, they were used to the idea that acquiring information is the best way of reducing the uncertainty of tomorrow. Far from being the population-oppressing exercises in world government imagined by our conspiracy theorist, these meetings are essentially a chance to get ahead of the curve by talking to other well-informed people.

But in the hour of the predator, this rule no longer applies. Today, we possess more information than ever before, and are less capable than ever before of predicting what will happen next. Our ancestors lived in far more data-poor societies than ours, but they were able to make plans for themselves and their descendants. We have ever less understanding of the world in which we will wake up tomorrow morning.

This paradox is not conjunctural, but structural. It is a consequence of the very nature of the digital universe. By reducing reality to a series of os and 1s, digital coding achieves its implacable aim of homogenization, eliminating anything that cannot be quantified. In doing this, the transition from analogue to digital glosses over the deeper meaning of things and flings open the doors to chaos.

This is why we have no future, at least in the sense that our grandparents had a future. 'Fully imagined cultural futures were the luxury of another day, one in which "now" was of some greater duration,' wrote the cyber-punk author William Gibson. For us, everything can change so suddenly that futures like those of our grand-parents don't have enough 'now' to last the pace.

A reality like this one is a reality in which only Borgians feel comfortable, because they feed on chaos. And God knows that most of the people present this afternoon in Lisbon do not feel the slightest sympathy for the Borgians, who are the stuff of their worst nightmares.

But here are Altman and Hassabis to offer them an alternative. The harmony of the world can be re-established in all its splendour. Artificial intelligence also feeds on chaos, but in return it promises a new order. A rational government of society. Data-based decision-making. Theoretically, this is a technocrat's dream. But there is a hitch. For the reign of AI to begin, we must first replace knowledge with faith.

Someone asks: 'Will AIs one day be able to explain how they make their decisions?' And the two tech overlords shake their heads. No, that will never happen. But don't worry, the models will be reliable. We just need to put our trust in them.

Like Kierkegaard's God, AI cannot be conceived in

purely rational terms. The only way of entering into a relationship with it is through an act of faith. Its great promise is to predict, even if we don't understand. The tech overlords don't see why this is a problem. Since they are not interested in history or philosophy, they don't realize that what they're proposing is equivalent to going back in time to the age before the Enlightenment, to a world of incomprehensible magic, where we will pray to AI as our ancestors prayed to the old gods.

'It's not always the same gods who reign in the sky, not always the same empires collecting their taxes in city and country,' says Moctezuma in his imaginary dialogue with Italo Calvino. He, and all those like him, resign themselves with good grace.

Kissinger is a tougher nut to crack. His body has deteriorated to such a degree that he needs help to stand up. And his cavernous voice, always famous for its unintelligibility, is now reduced to an almost inaudible gurgling sound. At almost a hundred years old, he could be anywhere he likes at this moment. Instead of which, he is here, in the conference room of this hotel in Lisbon, discussing artificial intelligence. Discussing its 'consequences', even, despite the fact that he is well aware he won't be around to see the vast majority of them.

Years ago, following his first encounter with Hassabis, he was asking himself the most difficult yet important question: 'What will become of human consciousness if its own explanatory power is surpassed by AI, and societies are no able to interpret the world they inhabit in terms that are meaningful to them?'

The novel that truly foreshadowed AI is Kafka's *The Trial*, in which nobody understands what is going on—not the accused, nor even the judges who question him—and yet events follow their inexorable course. In Kafka's other great novel, *The Castle*, when the protagonist, K, attempts to focus on the centre of power that controls his fate, the centre of power into which he cannot gain access or any kind of insight, his 'eyes could find nothing to fasten on'. And when he tries to telephone the castle, all he hears on the other end of the line is the singing of distant voices or, even more disturbingly, a cold, arrogant voice that refuses to provide him with any explanation whatsoever.

For some people, the Castle is already here. When we say that the future is living among us, but that it is distributed unequally, we usually mean that the most privileged members of society already have access to the technologies of the future, while others are still trapped in the past. In this case, though, the situation is reversed. The Castle is, for now, merely a hypothesis for the wealthier among us, but for those at the bottom of the ladder it is already a reality. Delivery workers, for example, have practically no contact with other humans in the course of their working day. Their only interface is with an app on their phone. It is the app that tells them what to do and where to go, and that assesses their performance, following a logic that can sometimes appear comprehensible and then, suddenly, completely impenetrable. If something goes wrong—if there's an unexpected incident or the app malfunctions— there is no one the delivery worker can turn to. The app draws its own conclusions and renders its verdict. The common sense and compassion of a human being have been deliberately removed from the process. At best, the worker can complain to a call centre, located thousands of miles away, where, after a long delay, he will be per- mitted to speak to another human as powerless as him.

As time passes, the Castle occupies new spaces and expands into other spheres of activity. The more the power of AI increases, the more the Castle climbs the echelons of the social hierarchy. If factory workers have been replaced by machines and delivery workers are increasingly being transformed into machines, the same phenomenon is now affecting white-collar workers and will soon reach the more learned professions: in the near future, doctors, accountants and lawyers will have to follow the AI's instructions and provide a justification whenever they make a decision that deviates from these guidelines. Only the most powerful will have any leeway, and even that may not last long.

The Castle is conquering new territories all the time, and perhaps what made Kissinger's friends look so alarmed was the foreboding that, one day, it will take over their lives too, once the crushing superiority of algorithms over the judgement of human politicians and CEOs has been demonstrated beyond any shadow of a doubt. That day, the Castle will have covered the entire world and the only ones who will be able to dance, free to follow their whims like those Saxon dukes of old, will be the priests of this new cult, the conquistadors of AI, who will for a moment taste the nectar of the gods, before being doomed to oblivion, like the rest of us, by the post-human matrix.

LIEUSAINT, DECEMBER 2024

A MID THE UNIFORM grey mass of the Parisian suburbs, there is a town of 14,000 souls, indistinguishable
from all the other new towns except perhaps by its pretty,
allusive name: Lieusaint. 'Holy place' in English. The
town's mayor, Michel Bisson, is a straight-talking, determined man in his fifties. A five-minute conversation with
him is enough to convince you that he has every quality
you would want from a local politician: deep roots and a
deep knowledge of the territory, a love of detail, a desire
to make an impact on reality, and the ability to resolve
conflicts, reconcile contradictory demands and make
decisions in an ever-changing context. He also has a fine
sense of irony, mixed with a small dose of fatalism. And,
of course, the necessary cunning, love of power and need
for attention. But what strikes you more than anything is

the pleasure he takes in human contact, in the warmth and surprises that contact with humans tends to produce. He is the very opposite of the robotic tech overlords and their obsessive drive to transform humans into machines.

Having been in the job for a quarter of a century, the mayor has seen pretty much everything under the sun, but a few years ago he was confronted with an unprecedented problem. Every morning, from seven o'clock onwards, at first a few hundred, and then thousands of cars would turn off the road to Paris that runs alongside his town to drive through the peaceful centre and the residential streets in the north of Lieusaint. Suddenly, a continuous flow of HGVs and SUVs would roar past the sleepy houses along the Flâche woods and the Ormoy canal, between the plane trees on the Avenue des Pépinières and past the recreation centre on Rue de Tigery, without even slowing down when they reached the childcare centre on Rue du Saule-de-la-Chasse or the Le Petit-Prince school. Well, not until they were forced to slow down by the traffic jams that began to form.

Within a few days, the peaceful residential streets of Lieusaint had been transformed into an urban hellscape: walking the kids to school became almost an assault course, with the constant risk of being run over and the din of honking horns, the road rage incidents, the congestion, the delays, the air pollution.

It didn't take the mayor long to work out that the cause of this disturbance was a smiling speech bubble on wheels, recognizable to millions of drivers worldwide: Waze, the Google app that suggests faster itineraries in real time, enabling people to save time and avoid traffic jams. It has been a blessing for drivers, like a giant godlike finger descending from the heavens to show them the way. Unlike God, however, Waze has only one mission: to save its users time. All other considerations are deemed irrelevant. If leaving the motorway to drive through a residential neighbourhood, speeding past nurseries and retirement homes, endangering the safety and peace of mind of residents, can shave even a minute—just sixty miserable seconds—off the commute time of one its users, Waze will unhesitatingly send them in that direction.

Just like its designers, Waze is so focused on its single objective that it is incapable of seeing the bigger picture. Anything that might slow down its pursuit of efficiency is just noise: useless at best, harmful at worst.

The mayor of Lieusaint has a slightly different point of view. Bisson is far from a Luddite. Years ago, he was one of the first mayors in the region to allow the construction of a data centre on his territory. When he goes home in the evenings, he likes to play video games. And he himself is a Waze user. But in this particular case, he could not just stand by.

After an in-depth analysis of the situation, he decided to change his town's traffic plan by adding one-way streets and lowering the speed limit to 20 mph. Then he put a traffic light on Boulevard de l'Europe, at a spot where it is really not necessary, with the aim of slowing drivers down by a couple of minutes and thus manipulating the Waze algorithm. The crux of the problem consisted in deterring commuters without causing too much hassle for residents. These measures had an effect, but they did not solve the problem.

Bisson decided to trace the issue back to its source, but soon encountered the difficulty that Waze is just like all other online platforms. A globally recognized brand, with hundreds of millions of users, a multibillion-dollar turnover and a massive impact on the life of towns and territories all over the planet. But if you need to speak to someone, there is not a single employee in France, not even a telephone number you can call. Just the hum of distant voices in the Castle.

As he looked more deeply into the issue, the mayor dis-covered that Waze is based on the work of volunteer cartographers who categorize the different types of roads and help the application develop a more refined under-standing of the road network. Once again, as is generally the case, the Castle appropriates a public asset and trans-forms it into private profit. With his fine political instincts, Bisson attempted to take advantage of the situation by approaching the cartographers and asking them to reclas-sify some of the streets in Lieusaint—into which the app was sending its flow of users—as rural pathways. The cartographers were sympathetic, but there was a limit to what they would agree to do. 'They have a certain profes-sional pride,' says the mayor. 'Perfectly understandable. They're doing this because they're passionate about it, so they can't just write something that isn't true.'

By this point, the only solution remaining was the nuclear option: to alert the media. Because, irrespective of what the new ruling elite of social networks and their masters might say, the press retains an ability to counter their power. Bisson, who is charismatic and media-savvy, spoke to several journalists and gave them his town's SOS mes-sage. The 'anti-Waze mayor' became a big story. This angle embarrassed him a little bit, since he is essentially pro-technology, but what choice did he have?

Finally, someone came down from the Castle. This was back when the platforms still cared about bad press. Since Waze does not have a French headquarters, a team of minions was dispatched from the European HQ in Amsterdam. In the conference room of Lieusaint's town hall, Bisson explained the problem to them. They were polite. They nodded understandingly and took notes. Bisson, who wasn't born yesterday, realized they were only there as a diversion tactic. It was clear to him that they had no power. They, too, were nothing more than cogs in the algorithmic machine.

In despair, the mayor asked them to at least make a few concessions. For example, why not take into account schools and hospitals so that they can be spared the heavy traffic directed past their doors by the app?

The Castle's emissaries listened attentively, nodded understandingly again, then politely took their leave. The mayor never heard another word from them.

After recounting all this, Bisson rolls his eyes. We are in the very same conference room where he met with the delegation from Waze. The feeble winter sunlight that came through the window earlier in our conversation has faded and been replaced by the artificial brightness of fluorescent ceiling lamps.

'Do you think they did anything?'

He shrugs. 'What do you think?'

'Probably not.'

The mayor of Lieusaint smiles. The struggle continues.

NOTES AND BIBLIOGRAPHY

PAGE VII.   Epigraph quotation Curzio Malaparte, from *Coup d'État: The Technique of Revolution.*

PAGE 3.   The introduction to this book includes a fragment from a Sándor Márai quotation that deserves to be read in full: 'Perhaps this world is coming to its end… Perhaps lights are going out all over the world just as they did today across this little part of it; perhaps some elemental event has taken place that is not merely the war, but something more; perhaps something has found its time in us as well, and now it's being settled with steel and fire, where once it was settled with words.' (Sándor Márai, *Embers*, New York, Vintage, 2002; translated from the Hungarian by Carol Brown Janeway.)

PAGE 6.   Mérimée, in Paul Morand, *Journal d'un attaché d'ambassade* (1916–1917), Paris, Gallimard, 1996, p. 64.

PAGE 10.   Flaubert, *L'Éducation sentimentale*, Paris, Gallimard, 1972, p. 352.

PAGE 12.   See José Ortega y Gasset, *El origen deportivo del estado*, 1966.

PAGE 14.   The game of percentages from TV shows is inspired by: David Sirota, 'What *Veep* Got Right About Our Government', *Salon*, 27 June 2013—online: https://www. salon.com/2013/06/27/what_veep_got_right_about_our_ government/

PAGE 18.   Vladislav Surkov, «Куда делся хаос? Распаковка стабильности», *Актуальные комментарии*, 20 November 2021—online: https:// actualcomment.ru/ kuda-delsya-khaos-raspakovka-stabilnosti-2111201336.html

PAGE 20.   Tolstoy, in Nicola Chiaromonte, *Credere e non credere*, Bologna, Il Mulino, 1993, p. 61. Chiaromonte completes the phrase in his own words, which I have translated in the line following the quotation.

PAGE 23.   Tony Blair, *On Leadership: Lessons for the 21st Century*, New York, Crown, 2024.

PAGE 29.   Alexandre Kojève, interview with Gilles Lapouge in January 1968, 'Les philosophes ne m'intéressent pas, je cherche des sages', *Le Grand Continent*, 25 December 2020—online: https:// legrandcontinent.eu/fr/2020/12/25/conversation-alexandre-kojeve/

PAGE 33–34.   See Francesco Guicciardini, *The History of Italy, 1492–1534*.

PAGE 35.   Leonardo da Vinci, in Patrick Boucheron, *Léonard et Machiavel*, Paris, Verdier, 2008, p. 99.

PAGES 46–48.   See Niccolò Machiavelli, 'Descrizione del modo tenuto dal duca Valentino nello ammazzare

Vitellozzo Vitelli, Oliverotto da Fermo, il signor Pagolo e il duca di Gravina Orsini', *Opere*, Florence, Gaetano Cambiagi, 1782, pp. 116–122.

PAGE 49. Niccolò Machiavelli, *The Prince*, chapter 3, translated from the Italian by N.H. Thomson (New York, P.F. Collier & Son, 1910).

PAGE 52. Tolstoy developed this theme in *War and Peace*. See also the excellent commentary by Nicola Chiaromonte, op. cit., pp. 43–82.

PAGE 53. Johann Wolfgang von Goethe, *Conversation with Friedrich von Müller*.

PAGES 56–58. The quotations by Nayib Bukele are taken from the speech he gave to the UN General Assembly on 24 September 2024, and from Vera Bergengruen's article, 'How Nayib Bukele's "Iron Fist" Has Transformed El Salvador', *Time* magazine, 29 August 2024—full text online: https://time.com/7015636/president-nayib-bukele-interview/

PAGE 69. Bismarck, in Henriette Levillain, *Saint-John Perse*, Paris, Fayard, 2013, p. 284.

PAGE 70. Cardinal de Retz discusses philosophers 'who have always counted for nothing [in politics], because they never put their hand to their sword hilt' in his *Mémoires* (*Œuvres*, 'Bibliothèque de la Pléiade', Paris, Gallimard, 1984, p. 817).

PAGE 73. See Janan Ganesh, 'Beware the Professional Ghetto', *Financial Times*, 17 August 2024.

PAGES 87–90. Yann LeCun, at the Night of Ideas 2022, hosted by Villa Albertine in New York—online: https://www. youtube.com/watch?v=f8js7OLig9U

PAGE 91.   Admiral von Tirpitz, in Peter Sloterdijk, *Zeilen und Tage*.

PAGE 91.   Curzio Malaparte describes his Parisian routine in: *Diary of a Foreigner in Paris*. The biographical elements are taken from Maurizio Serra, *Malaparte. Vies et légendes*, Paris, Grasset, 2011.

PAGES 93–96.   Curzio Malaparte, *Coup d'État: The Technique of Revolution*.

PAGE 101.   Amelot de la Houssaie attributes the quotation on dissembling (probably falsely) to Louis XI, in *Tacite, avec des notes historiques et politiques*, Amsterdam, 1721, t. IV, p. 113.

PAGES 106–108.   William H. Prescott, *The Conquest of Mexico*, Safety Harbor FL, Simon Publications, 2001, p. 487.

PAGE 109.   Joseph de Maistre, in Antoine Compagnon, *Les Antimodernes*, Paris, Gallimard, 2005, p. 77.

PAGE 113.   Francesco Cossiga, *Italiani sono sempre gli altri*, Milan, Mondadori, 2007, p. 195.

PAGE 115.   Kissinger, in Timothy Naftali, 'Kissinger's Contradictions', *Foreign Affairs*, 1 December 2023.

PAGE 115.   Churchill, in Henry Kissinger, *Leadership: Six Studies in World Strategy*, New York, Penguin Press, 2022.

PAGE 117.   Henry Kissinger, 'How the Enlightenment Ends', *The Atlantic*, June 2018.

PAGES 125–126.   See William Gibson, *Pattern Recognition*, London, Viking, 2003.

PAGE 127.   Italo Calvino, 'Montezuma', from *Numbers in the Dark*, translated from the Italian by Tim Parks (London, Jonathan Cape, 1995).

PAGE 128.   Franz Kafka, *The Castle*, translated from the German by Anthea Bell (Oxford, Oxford University Press, 2009).

WORKS CONSULTED

Giorgio Agamben, *Stasis: Civil War as a Political Paradigm*, Edinburgh, Edinburgh University Press, 2015.

BBC Television, *The Kingdom: The World's Most Powerful Prince*.

Franco Bernabè and Massimo Gaggi, *Profeti, oligarchi e spie. Democrazia e società nell'era del capitalismo digitale*, Milan, Feltrinelli, 2023.

Christian Chesnot and Georges Malbrunot, *MBS confidentiel. Enquête sur le nouveau maître du Moyen-Orient*, Paris, Michel Lafon, 2024.

Monica Duffy Toft and Sidita Kushi, *Dying by the Sword: The Militarization of US Foreign Policy*, New York, Oxford University Press, 2023.

Giulio Ferroni, *Machiavelli, o dell'incertezza*, Rome, Donzelli, 2003.

Antoine Garapon and Jean Lassègue, *Le Numérique contre le politique*, Paris, Presses universitaires de France, 2021.

Ben Hubbard, *MBS: The Rise to Power of Mohammed bin Salman*, New York, Crown, 2020.

Sasha Issenberg, *The Victory Lab: The Secret Science of Winning Campaigns*, New York, Broadway Books, 2016.

Brittany Kaiser, *Targeted: The Cambridge Analytica Whistleblower's Inside Story of How Big Data, Trump, and Facebook Broke Democracy and How It Can Happen Again*, London, HarperCollins, 2019.

Alexandre Labruffe, *Un hiver à Wuhan*, Paris, Verticales, 2020.

Jaron Lanier, *You Are Not a Gadget*, New York, Knopf, 2010.

William H. McNeill, *The Pursuit of Power: Technology, Armed Force and Society Since A.D. 1000*, Chicago, University of Chicago Press, 2013.

J.G.A. Pocock, *The Machiavellian Moment: Florentine Political Thought and the Atlantic Republican Tradition*, Princeton, Princeton University Press, 2016.

Carl Schmitt, *Machiavel, Clausewitz. Droit et politique face aux défis de l'histoire*, Paris, Krisis, 2007.

Deyan Sudjic, *The Edifice Complex: How the Rich and Powerful Shape the World*, London, Allen Lane, 2005.

Jamie Susskind, *Future Politics: Living Together in a World Transformed by Tech*, Oxford, Oxford University Press, 2018.

Christopher Wylie, *Mindfuck: Cambridge Analytica and the Plot to Break America*, London, Profile, 2019.

AVAILABLE AND COMING SOON
FROM PUSHKIN PRESS

Pushkin Press was founded in 1997, and publishes novels, essays, memoirs, children's books—everything from timeless classics to the urgent and contemporary.

Our books represent exciting, high-quality writing from around the world: we publish some of the twentieth century's most widely acclaimed, brilliant authors such as Stefan Zweig, Yasushi Inoue, Teffi, Antal Szerb, Gerard Reve and Elsa Morante, as well as compelling and award-winning contemporary writers, including Dorthe Nors, Edith Pearlman, Perumal Murugan, Ayelet Gundar-Goshen and Chigozie Obioma.

Pushkin Press publishes the world's best stories, to be read and read again. To discover more, visit www.pushkinpress.com.

THE PASSENGER
ULRICH ALEXANDER BOSCHWITZ

TENDER IS THE FLESH
NINETEEN CLAWS AND A BLACK BIRD
THE UNWORTHY
AGUSTINA BAZTERRICA

SOLENOID
MIRCEA CĂRTĂRESCU

THE WIZARD OF THE KREMLIN
GIULIANO DA EMPOLI

AT NIGHT ALL BLOOD IS BLACK
BEYOND THE DOOR OF NO RETURN
DAVID DIOP

WHEN WE CEASE TO UNDERSTAND THE WORLD
THE MANIAC
BENJAMÍN LABATUT

NO PLACE TO LAY ONE'S HEAD
FRANÇOISE FRENKEL

FORBIDDEN NOTEBOOK
ALBA DE CÉSPEDES

COLLECTED WORKS: A NOVEL
LYDIA SANDGREN

MY MEN
VICTORIA KIELLAND

AS RICH AS THE KING
ABIGAIL ASSOR

LAND OF SNOW AND ASHES
PETRA RAUTIAINEN

LUCKY BREAKS
YEVGENIA BELORUSETS

THE WOLF HUNT
AYELET GUNDAR-GOSHEN

MISS ICELAND
AUDUR AVA ÓLAFSDÓTTIR

MIRROR, SHOULDER, SIGNAL
DORTHE NORS

THE WONDERS
ELENA MEDEL

GROWN UPS
MARIE AUBERT